Why Are You Sick?

Why Are You Sick?

Practical Tools for Wellness

Francie Soito

Illustrations by Dawn Warren

Reiki Energy Healing, LLC
Milpitas, California USA

Why Are You Sick?
Practical Tools for Wellness
2nd edition

Library of Congress Control Number: 2019900881

Published and distributed by Reiki Energy Healing, LLC, a Limited Liability Company ♦174 S. Main Street, Milpitas, CA 95035, USA ♦ http://www.reiki-energyhealing.com

All client stories are used with permission. Some names have been changed to protect the identity of the individual.

* *Book cover design:* 99 designs by Arrowdesigns
* *Cover photo by:* wavebreakmedia/Shutterstock.com
* *Photo contributors*: Francie Soito & Maura McBratney
* *Interior illustrations*: Dawn Warren

Note: This book is intended for informational purposes only. The publisher, author and distributor expressly disclaim all liability to any person arising directly or indirectly from the use of, or any errors or omissions in, the information in this book. The adoption and application of the information in this book is at the discretion of readers and is their sole responsibility.

Dedication

This book is dedicated to my mother Marie and to my friend, E-Beth. Thank you for the lessons you taught me in life and in your deaths. I would not have started on this journey if it wasn't for you both. Thank you.

Table of Contents

Foreword

I'd like to share a story regarding a very special horse named Shaka. Shaka lives in Hawaii and for over six years suffered from a cancerous growth on her left hind leg. Her veterinarian kept shaving off the growth and was perplexed as to why it kept growing back. Shaka's owner, Rick, called my office in California and asked if I thought Reiki could help. I said, "It couldn't hurt!"

And after getting a bit more information I started to send distance Reiki to Shaka. What I learned from Rick was that about seven to eight years ago, Shaka moved from an area where she had a lot of horse company to a new property where she was the only horse up until about a year ago. When I started to send Reiki to her that first session, all I heard were the words *left behind* very emphatically. I got the impression that she was worried about her friends that she had left behind and about being left behind herself. After I'd contemplated this some more I put two and two together; it's her *left hind* leg that had the growth! Shaka's body was manifesting exactly what she was feeling.

I asked Rick to say daily affirmations to Shaka, assuring her that the friends she left behind were OK, loved and taken care of and that she was not going to be left behind. I sent the same messages to her during our weekly distance Reiki sessions together. Through Reiki I was able to also cut cords from that past trauma and remove any excess inflammation in the area.

As of this writing, Shaka is doing great and the growth hasn't come back! Rick had said that the growth usually comes back after about three weeks and so far she's beaten that record.

Shaka's story is a perfect example of why I wrote *Why Are You Sick?* Her story is one of hundreds like it that illustrates how our physical bodies show us clues as to why we got sick in the first place. Remember to look and to listen to the signs that our bodies are telling us every day.

* * *

Introduction

Why Are You Sick? is a practical guide to understanding the true source of illness and disease. Our bodies give us clues into what is truly ailing us, but we've lost touch with our ability to connect the dots. Breast cancer is a direct result of not keeping enough of your *love* reserves for yourself, of always giving to others until your tank runs dry. Lupus, fibromyalgia and multiple sclerosis are diseases of inflammation that result from your adrenal glands getting stuck in the *on* position due to constant, unmitigated stress. Allergies are responses to external threats that cause our immune systems to overreact to our environments.

    If you have a long-term illness, ask yourself, what happened one to two years prior to that illness developing? Did you lose a job? Get a divorce? Lose a loved one? Get in a car accident? Then look at your physical symptoms and see if they emulate this event. Did you develop a heart condition after a divorce or bad breakup? Do you suffer from thyroid issues that popped up after an event when you felt the inability to express yourself? Do you have digestive problems stemming from an incident that knocked down your self-confidence? Your body is constantly trying to communicate with you with every ache, every pain, every feeling of discomfort. *Why Are You Sick?* helps you listen to those clues your body is giving you and provides steps for you to take to be well again.

As a high-tech market researcher for nearly two decades and a Reiki Master, I've been able to see patterns emerge and repeat over time. These patterns show the link between how we think and how we feel. In these pages you will be given tools to help you see your own patterns, make the connections and learn to be whole.

My hope is that you will find the information and real-life stories in these pages to be useful. That some part of you resonates with what is written, even if it's only a sentence or an idea or a person's journey. May you find inspiration to take the necessary steps to be well again.

* * *

Why Are You Sick?

Red Rock State Park, Sedona, Arizona, May 2007

Chapter One

My Journey to Reiki

My journey began in 2007 when my mother told me I was supposed to be a healer, four years *after* she died. My husband and I were in Arizona on a much needed vacation. It was the first vacation we'd taken in nearly five years. We were burned out, and I was feeling lost, depressed and confused about what I was supposed to do with my life.

At that time I was struggling with my mother's death and the roller coaster ride her cancer had taken us on. It was a ride I hadn't signed up for; none of us had. If you have ever had cancer touch your life, then you'll know what I'm talking about. Cancer shakes you right down to your foundation. You begin to question your beliefs, and I was hard-pressed to make sense of it all. So the trip to Arizona was also a trip to heal and put some of the pieces of my life back together.

We took a day trip to Sedona and were immediately struck by the majestic splendor of the Red Rocks. They are as amazing and breathtaking as you hear people say. We enjoyed a lovely tour up to a church that was nestled in the base of one of these

Chapel of the Holy Cross, Sedona, Arizona, May 2007

striking hillsides. It was so beautiful and serene that I felt instantly at peace.

Later that day I felt a desperate need to reconnect with my mom. I missed her so much. When you lose your mother, it's like having the safety net that you've had all your life taken out from under you. There is no longer a sense of *home*. Mom was home for me, like walking a tightrope without a net.

Sedona is a spiritual mecca. The energy of the Red Rocks draws in intuitives, psychics, mediums and healers of all shapes and sizes. Being a researcher by trade, I didn't much believe in that sort of thing, but my wish to communicate with my mom outweighed my skepticism.

We searched all afternoon for anyone that might be able to help, but we kept getting met with

"Sorry, we're all booked up," or "We're closed for the day." We had given up and were heading back to the car when I saw a tiny sign in an upstairs window that read "Psychic." A little voice inside me said, "Go on, give it a try."

We walked up to the counter and asked if there was a psychic available to do readings that day. The stunning blonde woman at the counter apologized and said the regular person was on her lunch break. My heart sank as I felt my chance to reconnect with my mom slip away. Then she followed that by saying, "Well, I could give you a reading. I work with angels. Is that OK?"

Is that OK?! My mother *loved* angels. She had little cherubs all over the house and frequently called me "Her Little Angel." "Yes," I said, "that would be great."

The woman introduced herself as Doreen and showed us to a back room, where she had me lie on a table. She then proceeded to do an energy clearing in which she moved her hands up and down my body. I had never had this done before and didn't know what to expect. My husband sat in a chair at my feet and listened to what Doreen had to say.

Almost immediately, she was able to connect with my mom before I had told her anything. She described her in great detail: her loving energy, her smile and her favorite dog, Dusty, who was now with her on the other side. She even mentioned my mom's little brother Tommy by name, who had died in Vietnam decades before. I was overcome by emotion and could feel my mom in the room with us. The room took on a new energy that felt warm, comforting and

My mom, Marie Soito, December 2002

absolutely real.

Doreen then waved her hands over my hands, stopped, and said, "Do you feel that?" I was surprised to be able to answer, "Yes!" My hands got hot as hers hovered over them. She did this a few times, moving her hands back and forth, and I could feel the heat each time. She said emphatically, "You're supposed to be a healer and your mom says so too. She says you're supposed to work with animals and children. She also says to heal with your heart, *not* your head."

I was stunned, completely baffled. What the heck did that mean? What was I supposed to do with that?

Doreen proceeded with the reading, conveying additional messages from my mom to other members of my family and reminding me to stay connected with them, stressing the importance of family. My husband and I walked back to our car more than a little stunned but feeling very much at peace. We spent the rest of the trip discussing the reading and how spot on it was. The only thing that didn't sit quite well with me was the *healer* aspect. That was such a foreign notion to me that I didn't really know how to interpret it and was frankly terrified by the prospect of trying something like that. How do you even start?

Being a healer was the furthest thing from my mind at the time and honestly sounded crazy. Back then I was waist deep in data, literally. I was a market researcher for some of the top high-tech companies in Silicon Valley: Yahoo!, Macromedia and Facebook, just to name a few. My job was to find patterns in millions and millions of records in order to help marketers and product teams build the best products and market them to the right audience. That was my life for nearly two decades before everything turned upside down.

We returned home from our trip and jumped back into the minutiae of our daily lives: work, eat and sleep with little else in between. A year went by, and in that year I moved to another company and began working more intensely than I ever had before. My commute was longer, the demands on my time were greater and I again began to feel empty and unfulfilled.

As the stress began to mount, so did my health problems. When Sunday evening rolled around my stomach would revolt, forcing me to spend some quality time with my toilet. I was losing sleep. I was exploding at my husband over little things like not taking out the trash or asking me a simple question. I was not spending any time with friends or family because I simply didn't have the energy and didn't have anything more to give. I was miserable.

I was at the point of sheer despair when I remembered that little reading I had in which my mom told me I was supposed to be a healer. I reread my notes from that day and went to Google and typed "animal healing." Kids and I are a bit like oil and water, so I left that part out of the Google search. What came up first was a book called *Animal Reiki* by Elizabeth Fulton and Kathleen Prasad. I had never heard of Reiki before and was skeptical but intrigued. I went ahead and bought the book online, and it shipped later that week. When it arrived, I felt a bit awkward even opening the pages. I had never really read anything "New Agey" like this before. Was this going to change me into some flower child? Perish the thought!

I started reading the book and found myself unable to put it down. It was written in a way that was easy to understand, peppered with stories that showed the significant impact that Reiki had on animals. What struck me about Reiki was that it worked regardless of the practitioner. So I didn't have to be a super-spiritual person who meditated twenty-three hours a day, nor did I have to be tied to any specific religious or spiritual belief system. All the Reiki practitioner has to do is have the intention for Reiki to flow, and then Reiki takes over and does the rest. Reiki also didn't require a long training period. In fact, you could learn the basics in one weekend.

I read that Reiki uses what's called "universal life force energy," the pure energy in all living things. The "Rei" stands for "universal life force," and "ki" is our life force energy, also known as "chi" and "prana" in other cultures. This energy source has an intellect all its own and knows where to go and what to do. I found this to be completely liberating because it didn't require medical knowledge of anatomy or of various illnesses or ailments. This was also spot on with my mom's recommendation of healing with the heart and not the head because Reiki had its own guidance system, freeing the practitioner up to focus on compassion and love for the client. The philosophy of Reiki, which is similar to those of Qigong and acupuncture, suggests that if energy is moving through your body the way it's supposed to, then the body is better able to heal itself naturally. Stress, trauma and physical and emotional pain can block the energy from flowing as it should. Reiki identifies these blocks, removes them and then fills up the areas with pure, healing energy, creating a clean energetic state. All this takes place when the practitioner gently places his or her hands on the person receiving Reiki, with the intention for Reiki to flow. It is that easy.

What I found even more compelling about Reiki was that it was completely safe for the practitioner as well as for the recipient. In other words, Reiki works like a one-way channel. The Reiki practitioner doesn't run the risk of absorbing the energy of the person they're working on, nor does the recipient receive the practitioner's energy. I was elated to hear this because I knew that I was already sensitive to other people's moods and didn't want to absorb their emotions or even their physical illnesses. I have encountered a number of body workers, massage therapists, hair stylists and estheticians who are sensitive to their clients' energies and frequently absorb those energies, changing their moods instantly. That wasn't the case with Reiki.

Once I finished reading the book, I was hooked. I Googled "Reiki Classes" and found one in my area, signed up without hesitation and was on my way. At this point in my life I still wasn't interested in *becoming a healer*, but I knew I needed to learn some tools that would help me deal with the stresses in my fast-paced life.

I learned the first two levels of Reiki in one weekend. My goal in taking the class was to create a protective barrier to shield me from stress at work. My Reiki teacher was absolutely incredible, and my classmates were equally encouraging and warm. I learned about the history of Reiki and how it was started in the early 1900s in Japan by a Buddhist practitioner named Mikao Usui while on a meditative retreat on Mt. Kurama. I learned how to use Reiki on myself, others and situations. I learned how to send Reiki across time and space, healing things in my past, present and future and sending Reiki to people who weren't physically nearby. And most importantly, I learned how Reiki can clear up the energy in volatile situations and environments. This was just what I needed to help me at work. I felt alive, charged, cleared and ready to start using my new Reiki tools in my daily work life.

As I went back to work on that first Monday after my Reiki class, I felt ready to take on anything. Nothing was going to upset me; I was going to let it all bounce right off me. I was going to clear my work space and our communal spaces of any negative energy and all was going to be well. Or so I thought. As I took one step through the threshold I had a nervous breakdown. I started to cry uncontrollably and had to go straight to the bathroom to compose myself. I couldn't stop crying. I was shaking all over. What was going on? I had new training, new tools; why was I reacting this way?

After I was able to calm myself, I had an epiphany, a voice inside my head said, "You're not supposed to be here anymore". It was clear that I wasn't going to be able to make this work. I thought Reiki would be providing me with protection and shielding, but that day it did so much more. It provided me with new eyes to help me see more clearly. I was meant to do something greater with my life, and Reiki was helping steer me in the direction of my life's purpose.

Four months after that experience, I quit my six-figure salaried job, and four months after that I opened up my Reiki practice. It happened that quickly and was that easy. Life becomes a lot less difficult when you finally realize that your round peg will not fit into the square hole. I acquiesced to the thought of becoming a healer and, for the first time in my life, let something else take the reins. From that point forward I was letting Reiki be my guide.

But I wasn't just a passenger on the Reiki train. I did my homework, drafted a business plan, did my market research and came up with a solid business model. I found a great location for my office and lined up contract work from my old high-tech network to help support my family while I grew my clientele.

Everything happened just as it was supposed to. I slowly started to get more clients and learned something new with each person, with each Reiki session. As of this writing I have worked with over six hundred clients over more than two thousand Reiki sessions. I have provided Reiki at homeless shelters, medical clinics, corporations, and temples and helped to organize Reiki practitioners at cancer centers. I am extremely grateful for the opportunities that Reiki has provided my clients and myself. Through its powerful yet subtle energy, I've seen lives completely transform, including my own.

* * *

靈
氣
KEEP
CALM

AND

DO
REIKI

Chapter Two

Reiki, the Great Teacher

When a client comes in for a Reiki session, I take time to fully understand their goals for the session and why they came to Reiki in the first place. I have them fill out a short questionnaire as to their current mental, emotional and physical states as well as their aspirations for the session. We then sit together and discuss their goals while I explain Reiki and answer any questions they may have.

Next I'll have them lie, fully clothed, on my Reiki table or sit in a chair, whichever is the most comfortable. The sessions range from fifteen to sixty minutes, depending on the severity of the issue and the time available. I *turn on* my Reiki hands by simply having the intention of Reiki to flow and by drawing the Reiki symbols into the palms of my hands. I will then ask for guidance, clarity, protection and healing to take place.

With Reiki as my guide, I use my hands to clear energy blocks, cut negative ties, charge energy fields and help them return to their natural, healthiest state. This is a gentle and safe process. My clients will sometimes feel heat, cooling or tingling sensations as the energy blocks are removed and energy starts to flow again. They often feel peaceful and achieve a deep state of relaxation.

Once the session is over I have another discussion with them about what we both experienced. I will relate what I felt energetically, what parts of their body felt *off* and took in more Reiki. They too may feel things, places where my hands felt hotter or cooler than others.

Sometimes one session is enough to clear away the energy blocks. Sometimes a few more are needed, depending on the client and the nature of the issue they are trying to resolve. I've seen clients for several years as they work through different obstacles and aspects of their lives. I've seen some clients only once.

The majority of my Reiki clients feel great after a session. They feel relaxed, pain-free and clearheaded. When I first started my practice, I was thrilled with the results. Reiki was doing wonders for people and I was soaking up every minute of it.

Then I started getting emails and phone calls from clients saying that their pain, stress or sleepless nights would return a few days after their Reiki session. At first I didn't know what to think and was filled with fear; maybe this Reiki thing didn't work! I even considered giving them their money back. But at the same time I couldn't deny the miracles that I was seeing every day. People were getting better; I knew deep down that Reiki was working. But then, why were their symptoms returning?

One of my first clients was a woman in her late fifties whom I'll call Shirley. Shirley had been on disability for the last few years due to severe carpal tunnel in both her wrists. She was unable to use her hands at all: she couldn't write, she couldn't lift a gallon of milk, she couldn't open doors and she was in constant pain. Her first Reiki session was incredible. She was pain-free for the first time in years! In fact, she returned for a second visit four weeks later just to see if it was a fluke or if Reiki really did work. The second session went much like the first: her pain went away and she felt more energized. She kept coming back to see me once a month for a year. In between the sessions she noticed that the Reiki wasn't lasting as long, and she started to question its efficacy. I started to question it as well.

She was starting to get frustrated and I was beginning to sense, with Reiki's help, that there was something underlying her illness, something *behind* her symptoms. I started asking her a series of questions during our sessions, questions like, "Do you believe deep down that you deserve to be well?" and "What would your life be like if you didn't have this pain and were able to use your hands again?". I could tell that this line of questioning was uncomfortable for her. The pain in her hands was external to her; it was happening to her from the big bad world outside. In her mind, there was no way that she was somehow blocking her own healing or, worse yet, causing herself pain. Nevertheless I felt compelled to continue with this line of questioning as Reiki kept urging me on.

When she finally thought about it, she said that if her hands were healed she'd have to return to a job that she hated. This revelation was like a loud gong going off in the room. The air went still, and everything seemed to crystallize in that one moment. I looked at her and she looked at me and I could tell that only one of us got the message. Shirley wasn't ready to hear what Reiki was telling her. Even though the words came out of her mouth, she was still resistant to the concept that her way of thinking was preventing her from being well.

I saw Shirley a few more times after that, but we never again broached the subject of her role in her illness. It wasn't a topic she was ready to discuss, no matter how many different ways I tried to bring it up. Our Reiki sessions together became less and less effective with each treatment, and she eventually stopped coming to see me.

I had a fair number of clients like Shirley in those early days, clients with physical pain or work stress who hoped to find relief through Reiki. And they would. When they were on the table, their pain and stress melted away, but after a week or more, it would return. I had clients with insomnia who, after their Reiki sessions, would get some of the best sleep they'd had in weeks or months. But then their sleepless nights would come back. I had clients with migraine headaches who would find instant relief from the pain, only to have it return a few days later. I was starting to see a pattern.

They would tell me what their doctors had prescribed and other healing modalities they'd tried—massage, acupuncture, chiropractic, and so on—and those methods worked too, but only temporarily. They were looking to be cured using external means. Very few of them looked within to see what role they played in their own well-being. This was a revelation to me. Ninety percent of my clients, like Shirley, felt that their illness was some foreign invader, something that was happening to them from the outside world. When I would broach the subject that they might be contributing to their own illness through thought patterns and lifestyle choices, they looked at me as if I had sprouted two heads. And some of those clients faded away and didn't return.

The ones that stuck around used Reiki to help gain clarity into what role they were playing in their own illnesses. Light bulbs started to go on. Insomnia was traced back to a childhood when a drunken father would come home at all hours of the night. Migraines manifested from fear of seeing the truth. Upset stomachs came from a lack of self-confidence and feeling uncomfortable in their own skin. The inability to conceive stemmed from believing deep down that they were not ready to become parents. And on and on it went, with Reiki connecting the dots.

With each session Reiki peeled back the layers and revealed new meaning, new truths. Those clients who embraced this started to see longer term, more permanent effects. We were treating the root cause, not the symptom. How the illness manifested and its physical symptoms were clues as to what was really going on. Tumor sites in cancer patients pointed directly at the problem: breast cancer was a result of unhealthy relationships with themselves and others, gas tanks running on empty, giving and giving and giving from the heart until there was nothing left and their hearts would eventually break; uterine cancer was the result of empty nest syndrome; a rare blood cancer in which the white blood cells attacked the red blood cells mirrored feelings about losing a job and being attacked on all sides.

I started to understand the deeper power of Reiki. Real miracles began to occur when Reiki provided clarity by shedding light on what was behind the physical symptoms. The benefits of relaxation and pain relief were secondary. Gaining insight into the root cause of their illness was the first step toward healing—this was the true power of Reiki.

With this clarity clients were becoming conscious of their negative thought patterns and behaviors and were able to then take steps to change them. For some clients, shedding light onto the root cause was enough for transformation to take place. Others required additional tools and steps to help them on their journey of well-being.

* * *

During Reiki sessions I frequently get impressions of things my clients can do to help themselves. Affirmations, or positive sayings, or mantras are common suggestions, along with removing certain foods, people or places from their lives or incorporating things like yoga or mediation into their routines. Many issues stem from a lack of self-love, so I frequently suggested Louise Hay's book *You Can Heal Your Life* as a first step and a must-read for the majority of my clients. For those living in a "lack of" mentality, I recommend watching the movie *The Secret*, by Rhonda Byrne, or reading the Jerry and

Esther Hicks books, *Law of Attraction* or *Ask and It Is Given.* In some cases I refer my clients to a mental health professional or a naturopath or chiropractor. I communicate whatever Reiki suggests for them. Some of the suggestions are very specific to the individual and their issue; others are more universal. When my clients embrace these suggestions and gain the courage to make the changes necessary, complete transformations take place. Their physical symptoms diminish if not completely disappear, and their mental clarity and intuition reach new levels.

I began to see clients grow spiritually, becoming more in tune with their divine selves and their life's purpose. I would see clients who were initially shy and timid come out of their shells and embrace their full awesomeness. Releasing buried emotions such as fear, anger and grief allowed breast cancer patients to reclaim their bodies, replenish their hearts and find the strength to get through their treatments. Peace and grace came to those who were in the last stages of their life.

I am still humbled to this day over the significant, positive life changes that I have been a witness to through the power of Reiki. I have experienced something new with every client, with every session. I've learned to keep an open heart and to trust that whatever comes through during a Reiki session is for the client's highest and greatest good.

* * *

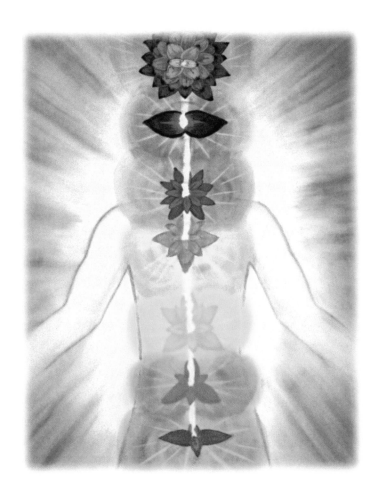

Chapter Three

Introduction to Chakras

Reiki works hand in hand with our energy centers, called "chakras." These "energy storage tanks" correspond to the physical, emotional and mental states of our being. Think of them as energy organs. Just as our heart regulates our blood supply, each chakra has a specific job or purpose in helping to process and move energy throughout our bodies.

Before we dive into chakras, we need to talk about energy. We are all energy. We are surrounded by energy; we absorb energy; we create energy. Every thought we have, every gesture we make, everything we say, think and do creates energy.

Just like our arteries, our energy pathways (meridians) and organs (chakras) can get clogged and blocked by either negative energy or a lack of energy. It's similar to having high cholesterol: if we have a bad diet and don't regularly exercise, our arteries can become constricted, forcing our heart to work harder to pump blood through our system. It's the same idea with how energy and chakras work in the body. Having negative or obsessive thoughts or physical, emotional or mental pain, or being in harsh environments or ingesting low-energy food, drink or other substances can create restrictions or imbalances in our energy flow.

Chakras first appeared in written text in 1200 BCE. The word "chakra" translates from Sanskrit as "wheel" or "turning." We have seven major chakras in the body that run up and down our center, starting at the base of the tailbone and moving up to the top of the head. Each chakra is tied to a physical gland in our body, which regulates part of our physiology like our metabolism, hormones or adrenals. The upper three chakras, located at the top of the head, in between the eyebrows and the throat, connect us with our spiritual needs, our higher selves, God, spirituality, our ability to see things clearly, our physic sense and our individual expression. The lower three, in the stomach, pelvis and tailbone, focus on our more earthly needs: food, money, shelter, addictions, power, sexuality and self-confidence. The chakra that joins the upper and lower chakras is the heart chakra, which acts as the bridge between our spiritual and earthly needs and represents the love we have for ourselves and others.

The more I worked with Reiki, the more I learned about chakras and how integral they are to our overall well-being. Chakras mirror our emotional, mental and spiritual states, our relationships to ourselves, others, the earth and the divine. When illness develops, it starts first with thought patterns and moves into the energetic field called the *aura*, and then into the energetic body affecting the chakras. Once a chakra becomes restricted or blocked, we can develop physical illness and disease in that part of our body.

During a Reiki session, people often complain about certain physical illnesses or symptoms. Each of the major chakras is tied to a specific part of the body, so by identifying the physical symptom first, we can then map it to the corresponding chakra. For example, neck and shoulder pain maps to the throat chakra, breast cancer to the heart chakra, headaches to the third eye chakra and knee pain to the root chakra. Once that is done, we can use what we know about that particular chakra to help understand what specific negative, obsessive or fear-based thought patterns or environments that are causing the problem. By using this method we can get at the illness's origin, allowing us to heal the entire energy system which in turn heals the body, mind, heart and spirit.

Each chakra has its own frequency or energy wavelength. The lower chakras vibrate at lower frequencies and the higher chakras at higher frequencies. These frequencies have corresponding colors, musical notes, crystals and essential oils. Once the chakra is identified, I'll recommend eating foods of a certain color or wearing clothing or crystals of the proper color to stimulate the chakra that is in need. I'll describe certain tools to help remove the negative thought patterns associated with that chakra, such as affirmations, meditation, tapping, journaling, visualization, yoga and environmental changes. I suggest steps that are safe and easy for anyone to try. These steps have worked with hundreds of clients over the years. They are meant to help create and maintain a clean energetic slate, allowing the body return to its naturally healthiest state.

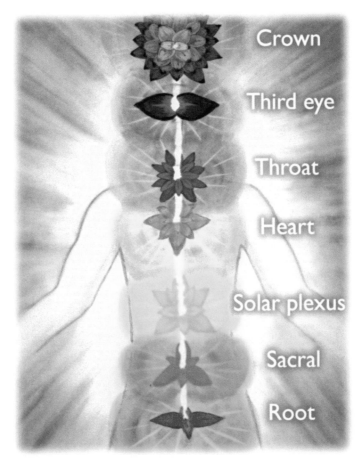

The Chakra System

Chakra Quick Reference Guide

Chakra	Physical Issues	Emotional/Mental Issues
Crown	Headaches, migraines, and nervous system disorders such as epilepsy, paralysis, Parkinson's disease,	Feeling disconnected spiritually, not connected to your higher self, feeling alone, lost, like a mental hamster in a wheel, depression
Third Eye	Migraines, sinus or pressure headaches, mental fogginess,	Being unable to see clearly, not sure of path, afraid of the future, indecisive; psychic senses
Throat	Hypothyroidism, hyperthyroidism, allergies, chronic sore throats, trouble swallowing, throat clearing, eosinophilic esophagitis	Unable to express yourself, speaking, communicating, feelings of not being heard, creatively blocked
Heart	Breast cancer, high or low blood pressure, heart disease, poor blood circulation, asthma, leukemia, myeloma and hepatitis, immune deficiency diseases like HIV/AIDS	Unhealthy love relationship with self and/or others, grief, heartache, resentment, giving until your tanks run dry, being unable to forgive

Chakra	Physical issues	Emotional/Mental issues
Solar Plexus	Stomach, intestines, pancreas and/or liver disorders, diabetes, gallstones or gall bladder issues, lower back pain, digestive problems	Lack of self-confidence, feeling uncomfortable in one's skin, body issues, feeling chaotic, struggling for control, feeling powerless, uncomfortable with your own sense of power
Sacral	Fibroids, enlarged prostate, uterine, ovarian and prostate cancers, kidney stones, fertility problems, irregular menstrual cycles, endometriosis, urinary tract infections and anything else related to the reproductive organs	Unhealthy addictions, appetites, desires, issues with sexuality, sexual abuse, inability to manifest desires, difficulty giving birth to new things
Root	Adrenal fatigue, fibromyalgia, multiple sclerosis, lupus, joint and muscle pain, middle back pain, leg, knee and foot pain, obesity, low energy, depression, insomnia, PTSD, inflammatory diseases	Concerns about finances, stability, feeling unsafe, unprotected, always on high alert, unmitigated stress

Getting to the Root of the Problem

Below I've listed the steps that I use with my clients in helping them identify the root cause of their illness. Using the Chakra Quick Reference Chart on the previous pages, you can identify the source of your illness, map it back to the corresponding chakra and take the steps necessary to be well again.

Step 1: Identify the Point of Impact

Where in your body are you experiencing pain or storing your stress? It will be the first thing that comes to mind. You might have more than one place pop up, just focus on the one that comes up first. If you have cancer, where did the first tumor *originate*? For example, if you have breast cancer the answer would be in your heart area, if it is sinuses it would be in your nose, if it's back pain it would be lower, middle or upper back. If you have a disorder that affects your whole body, like a blood disorder, inflammation, fibromyalgia, or multiple sclerosis, start with the root chakra and work your way up.

Step 2: Pinpoint the Source

Ask yourself what was going on in your life at the time the pain or stress first started or you received your diagnosis. What was going on in your life in the two years leading up to the first symptoms? Take notes on the first things that come into your thoughts. Examples to look out for are major life events like a death, job loss, divorce, car accident, relocation or breakup. When you think about these events, do you feel your body change physically? And if so, is it in the spot where you are having issues?

If you're having difficulty doing this on your own, it might be helpful to walk through this step with someone who knows you well and will be open to sharing their thoughts with you.

Step 3: Find the Corresponding Chakra

Match that part of your body from Step 1 with the Chakra Illustration Figure 1 on page 26 and the Chakra Quick Reference Chart on pages 27–28. Does the description of that chakra resonate with your feelings from Step 2 above?

Step 4: Jump to That Chakra Chapter

* Chapter Four: Root Chakra
* Chapter Five: Sacral Chakra
* Chapter Six: Solar Plexus Chakra
* Chapter Seven: Heart Chakra
* Chapter Eight: Throat Chakra
* Chapter Nine: Third Eye Chakra
* Chapter Ten: Crown Chakra

Step 5: Follow the Steps to Healing

Use the examples and the tools in the chakra chapters to help you be whole again. Choose the exercises that feel right to you. Don't force it; if it's meant for you, then it should feel natural and comfortable. It might take some practice, so be patient and try them for at least two weeks before you move on to another exercise.

* * *

Chapter Four

Root Chakra:
The Basics

Defined

The chakra that causes problems for most of us from time to time is the root chakra, located at the base of the spine where it meets the tailbone. The root chakra deals with our most basic survival needs: food, shelter, money, safety and security. If we find ourselves constantly worrying about things like money or whether we have enough food to feed our families or a roof over our heads, or if we feel unsafe, then we probably have issues with the root chakra.

What It Affects

This chakra is tied to major stress glands called the adrenals, which sit on top of the kidneys, in the middle of the back. These glands act as our most primitive alert system.

The adrenals secrete adrenaline, which increases our heart rate, tightens our muscles and puts us in a state of extreme mental and physical alertness. When we were cavemen and women and were threatened by a saber-toothed tiger that entered the foot of our cave, our adrenal glands turned *on*, activating neurons and sending messages throughout our bodies, getting us ready to either stay and fight off the threat or take off and flee. This is what's called the "fight or flight" response.

When the adrenal glands become overworked, they can incite inflammation causing the body to attack itself. That can lay the foundation for diseases such as fibromyalgia, lupus and multiple sclerosis, as well as high blood pressure, joint and muscle pain, middle back pain, leg, knee and foot pain, obesity, low energy, depression, insomnia and post-traumatic stress disorder (PTSD).

Why We Get Stuck

Many of us allow so many stressors to affect us that our adrenal glands get stuck in the *on* position permanently. When we see everything as a threat level *red*, equivalent to the tiger at the foot of the cave, we experience adrenal fatigue, paving the way to a whole host of illnesses and diseases.

Numerous circumstances in our lives that are outside our control can cause stress: getting laid off from a job, the traumatic death of a loved one, a car accident. What we can control is how we respond to these situations and how we let them affect us.

Client Stories

For four years I provided Reiki to women at a homeless shelter. During that time I saw firsthand how basic human needs not being met affected these women and their children. Uncertainty regarding their future and the future of their children caused these women a great deal of stress and anxiety. Imagine having ninety days to find a job *and* a place to live for you and your children or face being turned out onto the street, again. And these women were the lucky ones who had made it into the shelter in the first place. Often the center had to turn away people at the door because they were completely filled up.

We would first **identify the point of impact,** where in their bodies they were experiencing stress and pain. The majority of them developed lower and middle back pain, shoulder and neck pain, digestive issues, pains in their feet and legs and illnesses like obesity, diabetes, lupus, cancer, high blood pressure, insomnia and depression. We would then discuss how long they'd had their pain and when it first started in order to **pinpoint the source.** Some of the women had been battling these issues for their entire lives; for others, events like job loss, an abusive relationship, or sexual abuse had preceded their symptoms. What was a revelation to me was that being homeless was just another symptom. It was a result of one of these events, not the cause of them. Of course, being homeless just added to the stress and caused their symptoms to flare up more, but very rarely did I find that *homelessness* was the sole contributor to their illness.

We would work on a multitude of issues together, chipping away at the root causes, freeing them from past guilt, abuse, lack of self-esteem and addictions through Reiki, affirmations and visualizations, all tailor-made to their specific needs. Once we were able to make progress on the source and free them from their past, we would move on to their current situation of being homeless.

During our sessions together, these women would open up as they never had before. The Reiki energy provided a safe and supportive environment for them to share their fears and anxieties. Sometimes just the act of talking out their situation was enough to bring them a sense of peace and hopefulness. I spent a significant amount of time on their root chakras during these sessions. I would use the Reiki energy to clear away any negative blocks concerning issues with money, food, shelter and safety.

I had them try exercises to help them visualize what they want rather than what they don't have. I used visualization techniques and the law of attraction principles to help them attract what they desire rather than remaining in a state of *not having enough*.[1] I suggested that they focus on getting that next job and how good it was going to feel when they had a place of their own, a safe, stable environment for them and their children. I told them to *feel* as if what they desired had already happened, that they had already gotten the job, gotten the apartment. I encouraged

---

[1] Jerry and Esther Hicks, *The Law of Attraction: The Basics of the Teachings of Abraham* (Carlsbad, CA: Hay House, 2006).

them to bask in that emotion, that feeling of relief and joy. By feeling those emotions they were saying to the universe, "OK, I'm ready for you to send this to me now!"

For most of them this was an uncomfortable and foreign concept. They had been so used to living in poverty and struggling to get by that the thought of abundance and security was difficult for them. I suggested tools to help them: making a list of the things they desire, creating a vision board of the things they'd like to see manifest in their lives. Those who tried these exercises saw immediate and significant results. They felt more confident in job interviews, which led to more job offers. There was one woman who had been turned down for dozens of jobs who suddenly found herself having to pick between several job opportunities. Miraculous housing opportunities presented themselves, things like being moved up on a housing waiting list ahead of a dozen other families and being accepted over others with better credit scores and higher incomes. Slowly but surely, how these women saw the world began to shift once they recognized their power to control their own destinies. I would see more and more of them leave the shelter as different women. They had hope, a positive outlook and excitement for their new lives.

* * *

Another client story involved a gentleman in his forties whom I'll call Harold. He was worried about his ability to support his family once his work contract ended, and at the same time his landlord told him they had to move. During our Reiki sessions I could sense that his adrenal glands were in dire need of support. They were being overworked, and it was causing him lower back, leg and knee pain and extreme anxiety. I could feel the Reiki remove the blocks in his root chakra and recharge it with the universal life force energy.

We did several sessions together, and after each one he felt a greater sense of peace, followed by clarity on what he should do in his current situation. Once Reiki was able to remove the energy blocks in his root chakra he was able to quiet his mind and relax, which allowed him to see the steps he needed to take. Within a few short weeks he was able to successfully renegotiate his contract with his boss, and instead of finding another home to rent, he qualified for and bought a new home for his family! And his aches and pains vanished!

* * *

A female client in her thirties named Cara was desperate to find relief from her high anxiety. She suffered from lower back pain, insomnia and debilitating panic attacks. She had been to doctors and was currently seeing a psychologist. I felt her taking in Reiki in almost all of her chakras, her heart, her throat, her third eye and her root chakra. I quickly sensed severe abuse in her past and even had a vision of her getting slapped in the face. When I told her what I saw, she confirmed that she had been physically and sexually abused from her childhood through young adulthood. The trauma of these events was crippling her in the present. She felt like she was reliving these events over and over again. She was in a constant state of fear because she never knew how it felt to be safe and protected.

We worked together for a number of sessions, and during these sessions I would cut cords to her abuse, draw Reiki timelines to heal her younger self and suggest she journal, meditate, walk and try yoga as ways to free herself from the ordeals she suffered. During these early sessions, her body would shake uncontrollably as she released the adrenaline that had been stored in her system for all those years. Old, pent-up emotions would come to the surface before they were released, emotions she had buried over the years, like sadness and anger. Immediately following one of our sessions, she left to go grocery shopping and found herself purchasing a coloring book and crayons. She hadn't colored since she was seven. She went home and started coloring and found great relief in it. The coloring became another form of therapy for her. Her partner noticed a significant change in her, as did her therapist. She was starting to be free from her past traumas. Her sleep improved, her panic attacks diminished, her shaking stopped and she regained a fresh new outlook on life!

How Do We Get Unstuck?

Financial Concerns

When financial concerns dominate our thoughts it's easy to focus on what we don't have. The Law of Attraction states that we will attract whatever we're putting our attention to.[2] So if we spend countless, sleepless hours worrying about not having enough money to pay the rent or put food on the table, then we will continue to struggle with rent and providing for our families. If however, we turn that time and energy into focusing on living in abundance and envisioning the life we truly desire, then we will attract that energy into our lives. But it's not enough to visualize it; you actually have to *feel* it as if it has already happened.

For example, instead of being stressed about whether or not you can pay the rent, *feel* what it would be like to pay your rent each month with plenty of money left over to live comfortably. Take a deep breath and stay in that state. How does it feel knowing that you are financially secure, that there will always be more than enough? How does your body feel in this state? Can you breathe a little deeper and easier? Do your shoulders feel a bit lighter? That is the emotional state that you want to replicate as often as you can because it will bring the actual funds to you faster. And whenever you feel yourself going back to that feeling of worry of *lack of*, stop yourself and go back to the feeling of plentiful supply. And remember, there is always enough for everyone. Your desire for more will not deplete someone else's supply. There is plenty to go around.

Affirmations, or positive phrases that you repeat to yourself, can be powerfully beneficial when

---

[2] Jerry and Esther Hicks, *The Law of Attraction: The Basics of the Teachings of Abraham* (Carlsbad, CA: Hay House, 2006).

striving for financial abundance. Say phrases like these:

* I have more than enough money to pay all of my bills and live comfortably.
* My rent/mortgage will always be paid.
* Money is drawn to me like a magnet. I'm a money magnet.
* I deserve to be financially secure.
* I have a healthy relationship with money.
* I release any and all ties to poverty as I am living in abundance now.

You can place these phrases on your mirror and say them whenever you look at yourself throughout the day. And really *feel* what it would be like if these phrases were true. If this is such a foreign concept that you can't imagine what it would feel like to be financially secure, then just fake it till you get there. Use your imagination. Say them daily, and you'll start to see a positive shift in your mental and emotional attitudes toward money.

Do an image search on Google for the house you desire, the car you want, the trip you want to take and place these pictures in a collage on your computer screen desktop and screen saver. Use this same picture on your cell phone's background or lock screen. Stare at it often and breathe in what it feels like to actually have that house, take that trip, and drive that car. You'll be amazed at how quickly the Universe sends this to you!

Sometimes we feel destined to be impoverished. If our parents and grandparents also struggled financially, then we might find it even harder to break that pattern for ourselves and for the generations that succeed us. This was especially true for the women at the homeless shelter. We form ties or attachments to things, ideas, people, and places. Sometimes these attachments are good; sometimes they become weights that hold us back from reaching our true potential. The idea that your family has been poor for generations and that you too will follow in your ancestors' footsteps is unhealthy and simply not true. Worse yet, it continues to keep you impoverished. In those cases, cutting cords or ties to poverty can also be beneficial.

Cutting cords is a safe and extremely effective way to remove old ties and thought patterns that no longer serve us. I cut cords quite often during my Reiki sessions. You too can cut cords on your own simply by having the intention to do so. Say to yourself that you will break the cycle of poverty and that you will no longer be attached to that way of thinking or being. As you say this, take your right hand and move it from your left shoulder diagonally down to your right hip. Repeat the saying using your left hand to your right shoulder then down to your left hip. Envision your hands cutting through cords of poverty as you do so. Repeat as often as you feel necessary. Sometimes once is enough. If you find your mind reverting back to the state of not having enough and feeling impoverished, then repeat the exercise again. Use this in combination with the visualizations above and you'll quickly start to feel lighter and see a shift in your financial status.

As you are asking for prosperity, your role will be to look for signs of bigger and better things to help you achieve that goal. You might get a phone call from

an old colleague asking you to be .
venture. You might get approached by
to take on more responsibilities. Or you
call back from a job you had previously in
but never heard from again. You might a
see signs that you should further your edu   ... a
particular area, like seeing repeated advertisements for
a school that you were interested in. Or you might run
across people who start talking about that school or
field of study. These are signs that you are on the right
path. When you start to see signs repeat, take that as
a green light saying, "Yes! This way!" Keep with it, keep
your eyes open and remember, you asked for this, so
be open to how it may come to you no matter what
form it will take.

Safety

Feeling safe and secure is an important part of our
overall well-being. If we've had trauma in our lives in
which our safety and security were compromised or
violated, we can develop severe anxiety. This anxiety
can lead to panic attacks, middle back pain, sleepless
nights and other conditions mentioned earlier in this
chapter. The majority of my clients with severe anxiety
have had a traumatic event in their lives that has
caused them to go back and relive that state of panic
at the slightest sign of a threat. People with trauma
like car accidents, unexpected deaths, unexpected loss
of a job or home, traumatic divorce, war trauma, or
sexual abuse can suffer from these panic attacks and
may develop PTSD.

The first course of action is to identify the
traumatic event. What happened just before your

...ic attacks, pain, and/or insomnia began? Did something make you feel the rug was getting pulled out from under you? Did you feel as if your whole world changed, leaving you grasping for some sense of stability? You'll know when you've correctly identified the event because you'll be able to feel it in your gut. It's usually the first memory that pops up.

Once you've identified the trauma, journal how you felt before, during and after the event. Did you feel vulnerable, scared, alone, violated, angry, confused? How vulnerable, how scared, how confused did you feel? Do you still feel that way? When you think about the traumatic event, does your heart rate increase? Do you feel your muscles tense, your breathing shorten, and your fists and teeth clench? If you do, then you haven't moved passed this trauma, and it's still lingering in your body. The goal is to get to a point at which you think back on the event and it no longer affects you emotionally, mentally or physically. Write down everything you remember, everything you felt, without inhibition. No one will see this writing, so feel free to be as honest and open with yourself as you can. When you are done, you can ceremoniously and safely burn the journal with the intention of finally being free of the event. While you watch it burn, state that you will no longer let it affect you.

Another effective method for dealing with trauma is Emotional Freedom Technique (EFT), also known as tapping. Tapping was invented in the 1990s by a man named Gary Craig. He surmised, with the help of a clinical psychologist, Dr. Robert Callahan, that tapping on certain pressure points while saying specific phrases can reset and release trauma from the body. It's a way of reprogramming the brain so that when we think of the trauma, we become the observer watching it as if it happened to someone else. It's as if we become detached from the experience, not to the point of forgetting that it happened but to the point of releasing it so that it no longer affects us. The key to this method is making the phrasing reflect how you felt when the trauma happened. It's not enough to say, "I was stressed out when this trauma happened." **It's better to say,** "I felt alone, afraid and utterly terrified when this trauma happened." The steps to doing EFT on yourself can be found on Gary Craig's website: http://www.emofree.com, and are illustrated further in the following Sacral Chakra chapter.

During client sessions, I'll often use Reiki to draw a timeline back to a traumatic event. Reiki has the ability to work across time and space so you can pinpoint the exact moment of the trauma. With my client present, I'll go back to the point of the trauma and we'll use Reiki to heal that moment in time. I'll cut cords, freeing them from the event itself, and we'll heal the emotional and mental trauma associated with the incident. This technique provides my clients with the opportunity to speak to their past selves, telling them that they will be OK, reassuring them that they will get through this. This is especially powerful if the trauma occurred when they were children. To be able to speak to your younger self and tell them as your adult self that all will be well can be incredibly effective. It's as if they turn themselves into their own parents, guardians or protectors in instances where they felt there were none. For this technique, you would need to seek out a Reiki II or higher practitioner to help guide the experience.[3]

Affirmations can help you release a traumatic event and move to a healthier state of peace and a feeling of being protected and safe. Some affirmations for traumatic events can be:

* I am safe.
* I am protected.
* What happened to me does not define who I am today.
* I am stronger for having lived through my traumatic event.
* I can survive anything.
* I am no longer a victim.
* I will no longer allow that trauma to affect me.

Once we successfully overcome issues tied to our root chakra, we free ourselves up to focus on other aspects of our life that need our attention. It's difficult for us to focus on healing issues like self-esteem, heartache and spiritual growth when we're constantly worried about our basic human needs: food, money, safety, shelter, security. Once we are free from those fears and negative thought patterns, we become stronger and stand on firmer ground. This then allows us to tackle other areas of our lives that need healing.

* * *

---

[3] To help find a Reiki practitioner near you, visit http://www.reiki.org.

Chapter Five

Sacral Chakra: Appetites, Desires and Addictions

Defined

The sacral chakra sits within our pelvic area just below our naval. This chakra focuses on our appetites, desires, sexuality and connection with our body. Any issues with physical intimacy, sexual abuse and addictions are stored in this chakra. It is also the place where we symbolically "give birth" to our ideas and the life that we want to manifest for ourselves. It is a place for fertile thoughts and dreams. The sacral chakra is the energy source that helps us with these aspects of our earthly life.

What It Affects

When we obsess about sex, our body image, any type of addiction to drugs, food, alcohol, or other substances, our sacral chakra can become enlarged, darkened and out of balance with the other chakras.

This can cause us to have physical issues such as fibroids, an enlarged prostate, kidney stones, fertility problems, irregular menstrual cycles, endometriosis, urinary tract infections, uterine, ovarian and prostate cancers, and anything else related to our reproductive organs.

Why We Get Stuck

When our desires and appetites are out of balance, they can throw the sacral chakra out of alignment. Having unhealthy ties to drugs, alcohol, cigarettes, chocolate, sugar, or sex can overrun us, preventing us from being able to think of anything else but filling that addiction. These dependencies are merely substitutes for what we are really craving within: love, friendship, peace, clarity of mind, relief from pain. If you are in the throngs of addiction, ask yourself, what hole am I trying to fill? Is there a past trauma that you haven't recovered from, that compels you to numb the pain with drugs, sex, food or alcohol? Ask yourself, when did the addiction start? What was going on in your life that might have made you feel vulnerable, empty, hurt, and alone? And more importantly, do you still feel that way? By working through these emotions and traumatic events, you can free yourself from addictions as they will no longer be needed to fill the void within.

Our sacral chakra can also shut down and become blocked due to sexual abuse. According to the Rape, Abuse and Incest National Network, a staggering one out of six women have been the victim of rape.[4] When abuse of this nature happens, feelings of safety, security and trust go out the window. It takes several years of work to build those back up. Our relationships with others become affected: our ability to be intimate with a loved one and our physical abilities to have children may become impaired.

The sacral chakra is also a place where we symbolically give birth to things that we want to manifest in our lives. Creative or professional endeavors or things that we've always wanted to do or experience either flourish or die here in the sacral. Instead of allowing what we desire the room to grow and flourish, our fears and self-doubt cause it to shrink and diminish like a blowing out a candle flame.

Client Stories

Early into my practice I had a young woman in her thirties, whom I'll call Erin, look for relief from a sexually transmitted virus that she had contracted from an ex-boyfriend. The virus was getting progressively worse, and she was worried that it would turn into cervical cancer. Her doctors told her that they were surprised it lasted beyond a year, as she was in her second year of the disease when she came to see me. She wanted to try alternative treatments to stop its progression and wanted to avoid painful surgery.

When I first started working with her, I felt a deep emotional weight that she was carrying in her

---

[4] Rape, Abuse and Incest National Network, *Who Are the Victims?*, https://www.rainn.org/get-information/statistics/sexual-assault-victims.

pelvic area. The energy felt thick and heavy, and I used Reiki to sweep and clear the energy away and to cut any cords that were tying her to the disease.

We continued to work together through a half dozen more sessions, each time chipping away piece by piece at the emotional layers connecting her to her disease. She admitted to feeling depressed and confused for still having feelings for her ex-boyfriend, the one who gave her this virus. She felt ashamed and guilty, as if she were being punished for past mistakes. Slowly but surely as we peeled back each of these layers, she began to talk about her feelings, and as she did the emotional hold they had on her began to loosen.

Through our time together we also employed a few rounds of EFT, or tapping, to help her stop feeling like a victim. She also sought out the care of a naturopath to help her find natural remedies and herbs to help eradicate the virus.

Within three months, Erin came through with a clear test that found no trace of the virus. As of this writing it has been several years since I worked with Erin, and she is still free from the disease and credits her Reiki treatments and the help from her naturopath with eradicating the virus.

* * *

I've also worked with a multitude of clients who were victims of sexual abuse. One client in particular, whom I'll call Amber, stands out because her story was so powerful and profound. Amber had come to see me quite a few times and had attended my Reiki classes and chakra workshops. She was always very quiet, sweet and kind. She seemed shy, especially in group settings. She had come to Reiki seeking spiritual growth and felt stuck where she was emotionally and spiritually. She had recently ended a long-term relationship and felt lost and angry with how the situation ended with her child's father. Physically she suffered from irritable bowel syndrome, had gall stones and admitted to being an emotional eater.

When we first started working together, she noticed a huge change and an emotional weight being lifted off her shoulders after each Reiki session. She started to realize that the anger she felt was anger at herself for not speaking up and not expressing her feelings. In our fourth session together, she confided in me that she was sexually abused starting at the age of two. She said the Reiki had helped her come to terms with her abuse and that she unknowingly had let it hold her back and affect her and her decisions as an adult. She was ready to release it and wanted Reiki to help.

After she told me this we did a full Reiki session together in which I focused on her sacral chakra and cut cords. She no longer wanted to be held back by her abuse, and so the intention was to cut any ties she had to the abuse she suffered. After the session I drew a Reiki timeline, which allowed her to go back to her two-year-old self and talk to her as her adult self. This is an extremely powerful and emotional process and one that has long-lasting healing effects. When I drew this timeline I urged her to talk to her younger self as an adult and tell her what she would have liked to have heard then. Statements like, "It wasn't your fault. You didn't deserve this to happen to you. You will get through this. You'll be OK. This will make you stronger" came out instantly and effortlessly. She provided the support, comfort and security that she had desperately needed when the abuse was taking place. She was able to be that adult safety net that she had lacked as a child, becoming her own parent and protector. This allowed her to let down her guard and free herself of the fear, doubt and anger she'd been holding onto for all these years. She cried during this process, and with tears came release.

I have seen her several times since, and the transformation is amazing. She is a totally different person! She's outgoing, always has a huge smile on her face and glows with light and love. She has learned to love herself and to no longer let events in her past control her future. She's self-aware and no longer eats to hide her pain. She is vibrant, happy and healthy and embracing the person she is meant to be.

How Do We Get Unstuck?

Trauma and Addictions

When you are in the throes of addiction and sexual abuse, it is important to work with a trained, professional therapist to uncover and process the deep-rooted emotions associated with the issue. As with any healthcare professional, find the one who feels right to you, someone you feel safe with, who hears you and allows you to express yourself fully. It is a great sign of strength to admit that you need help and then to seek it out. Gone are the days when we need to suffer in silence or accept the judgment that people who see mental health professionals are weak.

Using Reiki timelines to go back in time and heal a particular action, feeling or event can be very powerful in healing the sacral chakra. Seek out a Reiki II or higher practitioner and ask them to draw a timeline to that part of your past that you'd like to heal.[5] Then, when you reach that point, talk to your past self, offering messages of reassurance and perseverance and comfort. Forgive yourself if that is what is needed; forgive others; let it go. Your Reiki practitioner should be able to guide you through this process.

Cutting cords can also be a powerful tool in helping release us from past relationships, events and traumas. When we develop a strong relationship with someone, be it a friend, family member or lover, we create cords of attachment to that individual. Think of them as invisible threads that connect you with the other person. Sometimes these cords are unhealthy attachments that individuals use to drain you of energy and become a burden and weight for you to carry. Other times we can develop cords that connect us to a particular event such as molestation or abuse.

During a Reiki session, especially with sexually abused clients, I'll often do a cord cutting, which severs any unhealthy cords that might be holding them back from experiencing their true divine selves. The act itself is a simple scissor-like movement of my hands over the body, generally down the center over all the chakras, not just the sacral chakra. The key to the movement is the intention, having that crystal-clear intention and asking for divine beings to help

---

[5] To find a Reiki practitioner near you, visit http://www.reiki.org.

guide the process of removing and cutting any cords that no longer serve the client. Cords and bonds of love can never be cut, so I'm only removing the unhealthy ones that are keeping the client locked in time or locked in a negative relationship. The process happens during a Reiki session and lasts a few minutes. Afterwards clients report feeling lighter, as if a weight has been lifted off their shoulders. Using this in combination with the Reiki timeline above, especially when dealing with abuse issues, can be an extremely powerful and effective combination.

Emotional Freedom Technique or EFT or tapping, as stated in the previous chapter, can also be an effective tool to healing past traumas and sexual abuse. It's a way of reprogramming our thoughts and severing our emotional ties to traumatic situations.

In Erin's case, we used EFT to help free her from the emotional toll that her diagnosis was taking on her. We started off by using the key, detailed phrase, "Even though I have this diagnosis and it makes me feel guilty and anxious and like a victim, I still truly and deeply love and accept myself." We'd say that phrase three times and then started tapping.

The first point to tap is at the very top of the head, at the crown chakra. Tap here repeatedly while saying the whole phrase or keywords from the phrase. In Erin's example we would shorten the phrase to the following "felt like a victim," "felt guilty," and so on. Then lightly tap just below the eyebrows where they meet and repeat the same phrase and keywords. Next, tap the outside corner of the eyes, then just below the eyes, the upper lip, bottom lip, underneath the arms and then the left hand from the side of the palm to the back of the little finger, the top of the ring finger, and the back of the remaining fingers. Stay at each point about fifteen to thirty seconds. Then take a deep breath and see how you feel about the situation. If you still feel your body reacting and your pulse increasing as if that situation was still fresh in your mind, then repeat the process again.

The goal is to get to the point at which you can view past traumas like an unattached observer watching a movie of someone else. The idea is to break that emotional tie so that when you think of a past event or trauma, you no longer react in a negative way. You can also use this technique to release yourself from addictions, fears, phobias, negative thought patterns and past karmic issues.

Giving Birth

The sacral chakra is a "birthing" place. It is where we conceive and give birth to our children, in both the physical and symbolic senses. This is where we nurture our ideas, our desires and the lives that we want for ourselves.

When I encounter a client who is struggling to become pregnant, the first question I ask is, "Why do you think you can't get pregnant?" I'm met with blank stares and then responses like, "I don't think we're ready to become parents" or "I'm scared to be responsible for another human being" or "I don't think I'd be a good parent because I didn't have one growing up." As these words come out of their mouths, they are shocked to hear them spoken out loud. Often they think, like most of my clients, that their issues are physical or biological. And what they often find when they leave my office is that their own perspective, their own mental and emotional state is what is preventing them from getting pregnant.

With Reiki we can remove the energy blocks that have formed from this way of thinking. Then they can start fresh with more positive thought patterns, aided by affirmations such as:

* I release all fears about becoming a parent.
* I will not let my own childhood prevent me becoming a loving, nurturing and supportive parent.
* I am excited to be a parent.
* I look forward to bringing another human being into this world.
* I am capable of giving birth to all that I desire.

Sometimes forgiving a parent for the trauma of a childhood can help remove blocks that are preventing pregnancy. Journaling the trauma or writing a letter to the parent involved and releasing it by safely burning it can help remove the obstacle to becoming pregnant.

Whether it's a physical birth or something in our lives that we want to *give birth to,* most obstacles to manifestation have to do with our fears. Fear of what will happen if what we desire comes to pass blocks it from happening in the first place. It might sound counterintuitive, but I see it with my clients on a regular basis. Deep-rooted fears that are just below the surface emerge during Reiki sessions. Fear of success if we try a new endeavor, fear of change if what we want to have manifest uproots our lives, fear of the unknown and fear of failure. Through Reiki, affirmations and tools like vision boards and law of attraction techniques, my clients can acknowledge and release their fears, allowing what they desire to come to fruition.[6]

Once we release our fears, we need to then trust and have faith that the Universe will provide for us, knowing that we are supported in all things. Often we need to get out of our own way in order for things to manifest. We need to learn to let go and be willing to receive the manner in which our desires come. Don't get tied up in the details of *how* it will come to pass, just know that it will at a time that is perfect for you.

* * *

---

[6] See "Financial Concerns" in Chapter Four: Root Chakra, p. 39

Chapter Six

Solar Plexus Chakra: Self-Confidence, Power, Control

Defined

The solar plexus chakra is located near the naval and travels all the way around to the lower back. In this chakra we store our insecurities and feelings of inadequacy, powerlessness, self-consciousness, feeling uncomfortable in our skin, anger, and helplessness. If you have ever felt victimized, as if the world is coming down around you and you have no control over the outcome, then you most likely have struggled with issues surrounding your solar plexus.

What It Affects

When our solar plexus chakra is out of whack, we can experience problems with digestion that can lead to Crohn's disease, diverticulitis, loss of appetite, nausea, irritable bowel syndrome, diabetes, gallstones, food intolerances and any other issues affecting the liver, pancreas, gall bladder, intestines and stomach. This chakra can also affect the lower back which can lead to chronic lower back pain.

Why We Get Stuck

Society has taught us to feel insecure about ourselves, our bodies and our capabilities. When we look at a magazine and realize we are nowhere near the weight of the models on the cover and would likely spontaneously combust if forced into a bikini or Speedo. Most of us aren't the perfectly fit models that flood advertisements. Even the most secure person can be rattled when looking at these unattainable images because it is in our nature to compare ourselves to others and to what we see in our environment.

We have been taught at a young age to look and act in a certain way, and this is especially true for women. We are supposed to be pretty, quiet, demure, alluring and the ultimate prize to any man who would cross our paths. Wrong. What we have been conditioned to believe is that we are only valid and beautiful in someone else's eyes, when the exact opposite is the real truth. How many times have we told ourselves or our children that it doesn't matter what other people think about us, that what counts is what's on the inside? Sound familiar? Yet how many of us still struggle with actually believing this?

Becoming comfortable with who we are, flaws and all from the inside out, is a truly heroic feat. It is not something that happens overnight and it is not something that can be told to us externally. We need to reach the point at which we can truly say that we accept and love ourselves, just the way we are.

But it is not enough to just be OK with ourselves; we need to also feel worthy of the thoughts, feelings and needs that we have. Being confident in our skin is also about being confident in what we feel and being able to express that without fear of what other people might think. We get stuck in our solar plexus because we have not fully accepted who we are as unique and powerful individuals with goals, dreams and ideas. We lack the self-confidence to express ourselves, to share our thoughts, feelings and emotions. When we suppress the powerful human beings that we are, we cause an energy disturbance in our abdomens that can lead to several debilitating and sometimes lifelong illnesses.

Next time you have an upset stomach, ask yourself, "Was it something I ate?" Or, "Is it because I have to do something I lack confidence in?" Pay attention to your body and journal what is happening whenever you feel your stomach is upset or you have lower back pain and see if it's tied to feeling inadequate or uncomfortable in your own skin. Also keep track of who you interacted with that day and what environments you were in. Your solar plexus can also let you know that you're in an unhealthy or unsafe environment.

Client Stories

A client I'll call Mary came to see me for stomach problems. Her digestion had been off, and she developed such inexplicable gas and bloating pains that she needed to take powerful pain medication. Nothing in her diet or lifestyle had changed, and she was a fit, healthy fifty-year-old who was studying to become a personal trainer. She never ate greasy or fatty foods, had a third-degree black belt in martial arts, trained frequently and was extremely active. The doctors couldn't explain the issues that had plagued her for nearly a year.

When she came in to see me she was distraught and tired of feeling poorly when everything she was doing externally was to promote her health. When we started working together, I felt a lot of heat radiating from her gall bladder area. A pattern I've noticed over the years is that the gall bladder is where we store suppressed emotions, specifically feelings of anger.

According to the University of Maryland Medical Center, fifty percent of U.S. women will develop gallstones by the age of seventy-five compared to only twenty percent of men.[7] Men are allowed at an early age to experience their anger, but women are taught to suppress it. For women, anger is viewed as unladylike and aggressive and is seen as a negative trait. Society conditions women to keep the peace, whereas men, through sports and competitive environments, are allowed to express anger and often are encouraged to use it. Anger is a normal, natural reaction to stress. If we suppress this powerful emotion, it will manifest in our body as an overabundance of bile, which is the key ingredient in gallstones.

---

[7] University of Maryland Medical Center, *Gall Stones and Gallbladder Disease* https://www.umms.org/ummc/patients-visitors/health-library/in-depth-patient-education-reports/articles/gallstones-and-gallbladder-disease, January 2018

Reiki was showing that this was the case with Mary. She had suppressed anger that was causing her to physically react with digestive problems. After our session was over, I asked her about how she was feeling and what was going on in her life when the symptoms first started.

About a year and a half prior to her symptoms, Mary's dad had succumbed to lung cancer. It was difficult for the entire family, and the way her oldest sister had handled the estate had left a lot of anger and hurt feelings. Her eldest sister was the executor of the estate and was controlling their parents' assets with an iron grip, leaving Mary and her other sister out of the decision making. This left Mary feeling angry, helpless and powerless. It had gotten to the point at which she and her younger sister were barely speaking to their eldest sibling, causing a huge rift within the entire family.

When Mary started talking about this situation, I could see her get physically upset as those emotions started to come out. I told her that her stomach issues were due to her suppressed anger toward her sister and feeling powerless and unable to express her feelings and desires. I could see a light bulb going off and her expression totally changed. She sat back for a minute and said that made a lot of sense to her. We talked about how she can alleviate these emotions by writing letters to her sister and then burning them and doing Tai Chi (she is a Tai Chi instructor), Qigong (energy exercises that use the body to remove energy blocks and increase the flow of energy) and more Reiki sessions. We worked on this issue together for a few more sessions, and during one memorable session the tears started to flow as she allowed herself to release the pent-up emotions that were stored inside.

After a short period and a few additional Reiki sessions, she was able to see her sister in a different light. She says that now she appreciates her sister for who she is, just as she is, free of judgment and expectation. Her parents' estate was finalized, and it ended amicably for all involved.

How Do We Get Unstuck?

Building Confidence

Confidence boosting is key for getting your solar plexus back in shape. It takes time and a concerted effort to work on building this back up because it's usually taken a lifetime to knock it down. The key words here are patience and persistence. Know that the techniques and strategies will take some time to penetrate that old way of thinking and have faith that you will have a break through.

Affirmations, like the following, are a fantastic way to start building up your confidence:

* I am beautiful just the way I am, from the inside out.
* I am comfortable in my skin.
* I love myself.
* My voice matters and is important.
* What I have to say and what I feel matters.
* I am strong and confident and can do anything I set my mind to.

Whatever your circumstance might be, you can find an affirmation that suits your specific situation.

Again, even if you don't believe these at first, just keep saying them daily while looking in the mirror and they will begin to take hold.

Making lists of things that you like and don't like can also be a great way to unveil thoughts and feelings that you might be unaware of. How can you be confident in who you are if you're not really sure who you are to begin with? This exercise is a helpful step in getting to know your inner self's likes and dislikes.

Take a blank sheet of paper and draw a line down the middle with "Likes" written on one side and "Dislikes" on the other. Then just start listing things in the columns that you like or dislike about yourself, your family, work and hobbies, as well as things you're passionate about. It's OK to write negative things down. Remember, this is a learning experience for you: no one else will see this. Get as specific as you can with this exercise, from things like "I like my hair color" to "I don't like the 1.5-hour commute to work." Really put some time into this. You may come back to it and add to it over the course of a week or more. At the end of this exercise, you might be surprised at what you wrote down in either column. From this point you can start emphasizing the things that you like and work on changing the things that you don't like with affirmations, visualizations and law of attraction techniques, taking real action toward improving things for yourself and your loved ones.

Another tool I like to use to build confidence is thinking back on all the things you have already accomplished in your life. Draw on your history as a way to help build up your confidence in the present. Think about a speech you gave or a test you passed or a trip you took or some other feat that you thought was insurmountable but that you got through. It might not have been perfect, but you did it and came out the other end and are probably stronger for it. Remember those accomplishments when you feel unsure of yourself and need a little reminder of just how awesome you really are.

Coming into Your Power

Once you have gained confidence in yourself, you can start coming into your own power. Our society has deemed being *powerful* as a negative trait. It implies that we are holding power over others. That's not what I'm talking about here. What I'm referring to is harnessing your own inner power to accomplish what you set out to do in this world. If you were put here to be a healer, then you need to draw upon your inner strength and power to make that happen. And it's no different if you are a teacher, lawyer, parent, or business owner.

You have the power within you, right now to create the life that you want to have. Just think about that for a minute. You have everything in you to build the kind of lifestyle you've always dreamed of. Through the Law of Attraction, we become co-creators of our life, which means we have the ability to change or create a new life for ourselves. As stated in the previous chapters, all you need to do is visualize what you want, the kind of people you want to have in your life, the type of environment you want to live and work in, and the contribution you want to make in the world. It's that simple. Now *feel* it as if that lifestyle has already manifested, and it will come to you sooner.

Push out negative thoughts and fears and allow your own inner power to surge through you.

Letting Go of Anger

Anger is one of the strongest emotions and is often the quickest one to surface during times of stress. When we're cut off on the road or feel lied to or cheated or in some way devalued or treated unfairly, anger rears its ugly head. Anger is one of the lowest vibrating emotions and wreaks havoc on our entire system, especially the liver and gall bladder.

When we swallow our anger and let things fester, it does more harm than if we were to process it and let it out of our system the moment it pops up. The key is to find a healthy outlet for that anger, one that will leave you free of the emotion so that it doesn't take root in your body.

The first step to releasing anger is to acknowledge that you have it. Think about something that you are currently angry about or something that you've been angry at in the past. Notice how your body reacts: Does your heart rate increase? Does your stomach get upset? Do your muscles tense? Do your teeth clench? If you have a reaction in your body, then you are still holding onto anger.

One of the best releases for anger is physical exercise. Getting the blood pumping and allowing yourself to work out the anger is a great way to release it—if you are physically healthy enough to do so. When you are exercising, have the conscious intention of working out the anger. Think about the situation that you would like to be released from and have that in the forefront of your mind while you're doing your cardio or lifting weights. Then think to yourself, "With every breath I release the anger I feel about this situation." Be mindful of your body's limits. Don't overdo it and cause injury!

Another favorite technique is to write letters stating how you felt or are feeling to the person or people who are involved and then burning them, releasing them from your body.

You can also talk to a trusted friend and explain the situation and how it has made you feel. Sometimes talking it through and getting it off your chest can help you to let it go.

EFT tapping, as mentioned in Chapter Four: Root Chakra, can also be an effective way of letting go of anger. Just remember to include a description of how you're feeling as you're tapping to make it more effective, such as these:

* Even though I was turned down for that promotion and it left me feeling angry, scared and alone, I still truly and deeply love and accept myself.
* Even though I am angry that I wasn't treated well as a child, I still truly and deeply love and accept myself.

And when all else fails, go to a sound-proof space where you won't be disturbed and just scream until your voice goes hoarse. I like to do this while music is blaring so I don't feel as self-conscious. You can also scream into a pillow. You'll be amazed at how quick and effective this method is to releasing anger. You might even end up laughing about it in the end.

* * *

Chapter Seven

Heart Chakra:
Love Relationships

Defined

The heart chakra is our love center. It is where we hold the love for ourselves and others, and it's also where we store grief and heartache. Because love is the key to all healing, this chakra is critically important to our overall well-being. The heart chakra, located in your chest and middle back between your shoulder blades, acts as a bridge between our lower earthly chakras (root, sacral, solar plexus) and our higher chakras (throat, third eye, crown).

What It Affects

If the heart chakra is out of balance, it can throw off the energy flow in your entire body, negatively affecting the remaining major chakras and your thoughts, attitude and physical well-being. The heart chakra is tied to the thymus, which regulates our immune system. Physical ailments related to the heart chakra can include breast cancer, high or low blood pressure, heart disease, poor blood circulation, asthma, leukemia, myeloma and hepatitis and immune deficiency diseases like HIV/AIDS.

Why We Get Stuck

When we have issues of self-hate or loathing we develop a dark and dirty heart chakra. When we are involved with love relationships that are out of balance and drain us, we can have slow-moving and depleted heart chakras. When we obsess over love relationship issues or become narcissistic, it can enlarge the heart chakra, causing it to be out of balance. When we suffer from severe grief, resentment or lack of forgiveness it can make our heart chakra feel heavy and weak.

Client Stories

Breast Cancer Patients

I have had the privilege of working with several breast cancer patients through my volunteer work at an organization called the Bay Area Cancer Connections in Palo Alto, California. There I organized several Reiki practitioners to provide services for their breast cancer clients on a monthly basis.

These women are incredible fighters. They are strong in their vulnerability. They knew what they were facing and faced it head on with guns blazing. Many shed tears and many more left their Reiki sessions feeling uplifted by a new sense of hope and peace.

While working with these women, I discovered a pattern that permeated the entire group. These women's heart chakras were drained. They were givers; they gave and gave and gave until their tanks ran dry. They gave so much that they depleted their own stores, which left them vulnerable to illness. They, like many of us, put their family, children and career first and found themselves to be tenth, eleventh or lower on their priority list, if they were on the list at all. Through Reiki and the incredible work at the Bay Area Cancer Connections, they were able to put themselves first on that list. For some of them this was a foreign concept, but it was a necessary step for them to take in order to heal themselves. They had to be the focus of their recovery. Their healing had to take center stage in order for them to be well again.

Many of them felt guilty for having this attitude as they believed strongly that they had to do for others and weren't used to others taking care of them. It was a critical and necessary mental shift for some of them, and once they took that leap their healing accelerated. They were better able to articulate what they wanted, when, and they were able to vocalize their boundaries of what they would and wouldn't do and who they'd do it with.

Once they realized that they were important and that their lives mattered they started to take charge of their healing. They went to group therapy discussions where they talked about how their illness made them feel emotionally, mentally, spiritually and physically. They changed their diets, taking out unhealthy foods and substituting antioxidant-rich foods. And they came to Reiki sessions and guided meditation classes and focused on fighting their disease.

During these Reiki sessions I saw a calming release come over them. They were able to let go of the emotions they were holding onto so tightly, releasing the fear, the anger, the exhaustion that the disease and the treatments put them through. Reiki was extremely beneficial in helping them gain back their energy, calm their nausea, increase their appetite and restore their mental clarity. Reiki seemed to help direct the medicine to the tumor sites and minimize the side effects on the healthier tissues in the body. Before their Reiki sessions they would look sullen and quiet; after their sessions they brightened up and left with smiles and a new sense of hope and peace.

Grief

Grief is like a scar that never fully heals. A scab grows over the wound, but it only takes a scratch to make it bleed again.

Grief has become my old familiar friend. It's my constant companion that butts in at inappropriate times: dinner at restaurants, the grocery store, hospitals and just about any place it feels like. It comes without warning, and it comes without inhibition. I've learned to live with this constant roommate, and as I've done so it's taught me invaluable lessons.

A year and a few months after my mom died, my best friend Elisabeth was killed in a car accident at the age of thirty-two. She and her husband were driving home from dinner when they were hit by another driver who ran a red light while talking on a cell phone. E-Beth, as we lovingly called her, was the definition of life. She was vibrant, excited and always looking forward to what the next day had to offer. She was a chiropractor and a true healer, one who

E-Beth and I at Disneyland, Disneyland, California, October 2004

intuitively knew what was wrong and always healed from the heart. When she would give you an adjustment, your whole body would tingle and then settle into a calming warmness. I knew E-Beth had a gift beyond her medical training, a natural gift of healing.

I had dinner with E-Beth a few nights before she died. She had been telling me about a patient of hers whom she had been treating for injuries caused by a car accident. During the initial examination E-Beth had found other, more chronic problems with the woman's lower back, separate from the accident. Elisabeth proceeded to set up treatment plans for both problems. Unbeknownst to E-Beth, the woman had been having trouble conceiving. She and her husband had tried for several years to get pregnant, to no avail. Her doctor had told her to give up and consider adoption. After only two short months of being treated by E-Beth, the woman became pregnant. Both E-Beth and her patient were shocked and thrilled with the results. It was just another in a slew of stories she had told me over the years in which healing miracles occurred at her hands. E-Beth left a huge healing void in this world, and I will never forget the significance of her healing story that night.

E-Beth's passing so suddenly and so soon after my mom's death sent me into a grief spiral. My heart felt physically heavy, and I couldn't take deep breaths. Nothing about the world made any sense to me anymore. My mom's death, though heartbreaking, was somewhat bearable because she had lived her life. She was in her sixties; she'd raised her children and accomplished what she wanted to do. E-Beth was just starting to live her dreams. She and her husband Stone had just opened their chiropractic office a few years before, and it was just starting to take off. We had made plans to go to Paris together, to take more Disneyland trips together, to grow old together.

Losing her was unbearable and too much for me to deal with on my own, so I sought the help of a grief counselor. I've never been of the mindset that seeking psychological help meant that you are weak or unstable. Quite the opposite: I find that asking for help and taking the steps to get it shows a great deal of strength. During our sessions, the counselor helped me put E-Beth's life in perspective. It was her life and her legacy that I needed to focus on, not her leaving us. The psychologist helped me talk through my feelings and my fears.

When you have a peer leave you so suddenly, you start to question your life and the legacy that you'll leave behind if you were to die tomorrow. It got me thinking about the void that E-Beth left in the world and if there was any way I could try to help fill that absence. It propelled me to think about what contribution I could make. E-Beth helped heal hundreds of patients in her short time on this earth; what legacy would I leave if my life was cut short?

Fast forward a few years to when I opened up my Reiki practice and I finally found a release for the grief I had been stockpiling for the previous five years. These two profound deaths in my life, so close together, compelled me to reexamine my own life and gave me the courage to do what I was put here on this earth to do, help others be well again. And as I started taking on more and more clients and saw them getting well and beginning to change their own lives, I felt that my mom and E-Beth's deaths now had purpose. I had used my grief and feelings of loss to propel myself into helping others. With each client I felt that I was honoring the legacy that my mom and E-Beth left behind. Finding my life purpose and living my life fully and completely was how I honored their lives and gave their deaths meaning.

Love Relationships

At least half of the clients I work with are involved in unhealthy relationships. Sometimes these unhealthy relationships are with themselves: self-loathing and self-hate permeate their being and block any kind of healing. Often these issues stem from being abused or constantly ridiculed from childhood through adulthood. Some are not happy with how they look, their life choices, their current situations or their current partner. A lot of times they aren't even aware of their own lack of self-worth and self-love. They will blame external things for their current misery—an unsatisfying job, their partner, their family or friends or their illness—when in fact they are just masking their true feelings of being unfulfilled and unhappy with themselves.

A client and Reiki student of mine whom I'll call Terry struggled with shortness of breath and frequent asthma attacks. During her first Reiki class with me she had a severe asthma attack while she was receiving Reiki. It was so profound that her emergency inhaler didn't work, which had only happened two other times in her life. The other two times were under severe fear and anxiety. She realized then that her symptoms were beyond physical, that there was more to it; otherwise her emergency inhaler would have worked. The Reiki was bringing her issues to the surface, issues that she needed to release. She was able to breathe again normally during the remainder of the class, and I suggested she come back to see me for follow-up sessions to help her work through her issues.

As we started working together, anxiety from her current relationship began to surface. Her spouse was draining her and she realized his attachment to her was unhealthy. It literally felt like a hook was placed on her heart and he was dragging her along with him. Over the course of several months working with a counselor and in regular Reiki sessions, she realized that she could no longer stay in her current relationship and got a divorce.

The more we started working together, the more she started to notice patterns in her relationships. She began to see the connection between her asthma attacks and the unhealthy relationships she was in. She traced it back to feelings of being alone and abandoned. At the age of eighteen she moved out to another state to work as a nanny, with no support system and no family to rely on. That's when her asthma attacks became more acute. Later on, Terry felt emotionally abandoned by her husband, which triggered her asthma again.

While taking Reiki classes and doing spiritual development work on herself, Terry realized that she was never alone and that God would always be with her. When that began to truly resonate with her, her feelings of abandonment and being alone went away, along with her asthma. Terry is now in a healthy, happy and nurturing relationship and is asthma-free!

How Do We Get Unstuck?

For Issues of the Heart

For all issues related to the heart I recommend cord cutting.[8] It is safe, easy and extremely effective in helping you let go of things that are no longer healthy for you. Having that intention for the unhealthy cords to be cut is the key to this technique. Remember, cords of love can never be cut, only those that no longer serve our highest good. You can seek out a Reiki practitioner to help you with this or ask God or your higher self to cut these cords for you. And for your part, you truly need to be in a place to let go. If you allow that person or that situation back into your life in an unhealthy manner, those cords will re-attach and you'll be back to square one.

---

[8] See Chapter Five: Sacral Chakra, p. 55

Rose quartz is a beautiful, soothing crystal that resonates strongly with the heart chakra. It can bring a sense of peace, calm and profound love. There are various ways to employ crystals for healing purposes. You can sit in quiet meditation with these crystals in your hands and contemplate the heart issue that you would like healed. You can lie flat on your back and place the rose quartz directly over your heart chakra, with that same intention of healing and letting go. You can wear crystals in a bracelet, earrings or necklace. You can place the crystal near your head when you sleep, either under your pillow or on a headboard. You can simply place them in your pocket and carry them around with you during the day. Let them speak to you, and try a few different methods until you find the one that feels right to you.

Whenever you choose your crystals, know where and how they are harvested. Crystals carry energy, so you want to ensure that they were extracted and handled in a careful and respectful manner. See which one feels right to you. Which one do you pick up again? Which one are you having trouble putting back down? Those are the crystals to take home with you.

Always treat crystals with a great deal of respect. Place them in sacred, protected places and cleanse and clear them regularly. You can use sage smoke to clear them or place them outside during a full moon or bury them in the earth overnight. Try to do this at least once a month, if not more often if you feel they're getting full.

Lack of Self-Love

When dealing with a lack of self-love, affirmations can be a tremendously powerful tool to help overcome those negative feelings. Phrases like the ones below can be incredibly effective:

* I love myself, truly, deeply, just as I am, right now.
* I am worthy of love.
* I am the embodiment of love.
* I love fully.
* I am loved for who I am, right now.

Make sure to say them often while looking at yourself in the mirror. And remember, it's OK to say it if you don't believe it at first. Over time, you will!

Another fun exercise you can do is to take yourself out on dates. Go out and treat yourself to a movie, massage, museum, concert, hike or something else that you enjoy. You'll find that you are better company than you might think! Really listen to what you desire moment to moment and be spontaneous; you might just learn something new about yourself along the way.

I also highly recommend Louise Hay's book *You Can Heal Your Life*. It helps put into perspective the power of self-love and provides additional practical steps on how to truly love yourself.

Grief

Finding outlets for your grief will help reduce untimely outbursts and give you back some control over when you break down. Find a super-sad movie, send the kids off to a play date, snuggle up with a box of tissues and let the tears come. Give yourself permission to have the ugly cry in the sanctity of your home. Think about all the things you could have done, should have done or said, and let all those emotions wash over you. Remember the good times and the bad and the final moments of your time with your lost loved one and grieve. It is normal and natural to grieve those that we care about. Let it out: no one is watching, and the more you let it out the lighter your chest will feel. Repeat as often as necessary.

I find journaling to be incredibly healing when I am in the throes of grief. Write letters to your lost loved ones in your journal. They will see it. Pour your heart out, rewrite painful memories, relive happy memories, be angry, be sad, be scared, be honest and pour it all out onto the page. When you journal you unburden your body of your emotions and transfer them onto the page. Again, after you do so, you should feel a weight being lifted off your chest. You can also safely burn the journal or letters as a symbolic way of releasing them completely.

Channel your grief energy into something productive and worthwhile in memory of the person you lost. Do a charity walk in their memory, volunteer at a homeless shelter if that's something they were passionate about, or bake a casserole for a friend because that's what your loved one would have done. Find the hole that they left behind: what does the world no longer have because your loved one is no longer there to provide it? Then pick up that torch and do it yourself as best as you can. You'll find that by doing what they did, you will become closer to them and their spirit will live on through you.

* * *

Chapter Eight

Throat Chakra:
Expression and Communication

Defined

The throat chakra, located right below the Adam's apple, is associated with our ability to communicate and express ourselves. Have you ever felt like you just can't get the words out and that no one understands you? Most of us encounter this feeling at some point, whether it's in our personal or work lives or both. Being unable to express ourselves verbally or creatively can cause us to close off from the world and suppress our thoughts and emotions.

What It Affects

If we stifle our unique voice, we can develop physical ailments tied to the very thing that gives us that voice, the throat. The throat chakra is tied to our thyroid, which controls energy production, makes protein, and regulates hormones, weight and our moods. Ailments such as hypothyroidism, hyperthyroidism, depression, chronic fatigue, obesity, allergies, chronic sore throats, trouble swallowing or a constant need to clear the throat can develop when this chakra is out of balance. These conditions will continue to afflict us if we are unable to express ourselves or feel that we are not being heard.

Why We Get Stuck

There are many reasons why we struggle with our throat chakras. We worry about being judged by others for saying or expressing what we're thinking. We lack the self-confidence and courage to be true to who we really are. We've had feelings of being ignored or unheard, so we suppress our voices. We've been told that being creative is not valuable and thus we stifle our imaginative side. Our ability to express ourselves and communicate effectively is critical to our overall health and well-being, and when we can't do so, the energy flow to this area can get stuck.

Client Stories

I've struggled with throat issues all of my life. Since the age of seven I've had chronic swallowing and choking episodes. It started with a large pill I had to take when I was young. It was too big for me to swallow, and it got stuck. My mom had to give me slices of bread to push it down. As I grew older, the choking incidents continued. It got to be so frequent that my mom was performing the Heimlich on me every other week. The doctors couldn't figure out what was wrong, and I was told to "chew more" and to "slow down" while I was eating. I took numerous allergy tests and did several food journals to try and pinpoint what triggered it, to no avail. I remember my mom taking me to do a barium test when I was about eight or nine years old. They gave me this terrible strawberry goop and then took x-rays while I drank it. The results showed nothing, and I continued to choke well into my teens, twenties and thirties. At times it was debilitating, causing me to fear every bite of food I put into my mouth. Was I going to choke today? What happens if I choke when I'm by myself or out in public? I started to blame and hate myself for this defect. What was wrong with me? Was it all just in my head, as some people suggested? I became resentful of my body for turning on me and developed a fear of food that caused me to remain small and thin for the majority of my life.

I can't adequately convey how dark I felt when my constant choking was at its height. You have to eat to live. It wasn't something I could avoid, and I had to do it several times a day. I developed extreme anxiety that resulted in an inability to digest food, which resulted in frequent upset stomachs. I learned to live with it and so did my husband, who had now taken over the Heimlich duties from my mother. It was affecting not only me but my relationships. My husband was and still is a rock of support. He held me during those times when I was completely devastated and feeling hopeless and helpless. Instead of being an integral part of our relationship, I was short-tempered, closed off and frustrated, and those around me felt that sting.

The only pattern I could see was that I was more prone to choke if I was under a lot of stress. One memorable incident happened when I was at one of my high-tech jobs. We were under a lot of pressure to get a particular project out, and every minute was jam-packed with things to do. During a five-minute break I took to gobble down my lunch, an employee rushed in to tell me about the latest fire that I needed to put out. As I was eating, I could feel that the food was becoming harder and harder to swallow, so I took a minute to excuse myself and went to the womens' restroom. Over the years I had learned to notice the early signs of choking: rushed heartbeat, painful and difficult swallowing and an instant loss of appetite. If I could recognize these signs early enough, I could prevent the actual choking from occurring. In my case, the choking was strictly in the esophagus. Thankfully, it never affected my ability to breathe, but it was still very scary and some of the worst pain I've ever felt.

While I was in the restroom trying to compose and calm myself, I heard the womens' bathroon door open. In walked that same employee from the break room who proceeded to cry out at me while I was in a stall. At that point, my throat seized up and whatever was still trying to pass through was in full revolt. Nothing was moving, and the pain and panic started. I couldn't talk and no one at work knew of my condition, leaving me feeling extremely helpless and embarrassed. When they noticed something was wrong, they called an ambulance and rushed me to the hospital. I remember the ambulance driver trying to get me to drink water and it came right back out— nothing was getting through. When I got to the hospital, the doctor just looked at me and told me to chew better. I still have that hospital release form from that day with the prescription "Chew well, eat slowly" from the attending doctor.

Years went by, with the same kinds of incidents, and I was growing more and more depressed and hopeless. Then one morning, as I was getting ready for work, I took a gulp of water and my throat seized up instantly. This had never happened to me before. Whenever I had choked previously, food was getting lodged in my esophagus. This time it was just water. How was this possible? I tried to take a few more sips, and the same thing happened. My throat was completely closed. I could barely speak, and the pain was unbearable. I was terrified and tried to make sense of this new horror. My husband had already left for work, and I was completely alone. I remember getting down on my knees and praying in complete desperation, "Please God, please, make this stop. Please help me be rid of this once and for all!" I somehow managed to call 911 and whisper out that I needed an ambulance. Within minutes the ambulance arrived and I was rushed to the ER.

It is in those moments of sheer desperation that miracles happen. In the back of the ambulance I felt an overwhelming sense of calm and knew that everything would be all right. I knew this new sense of peace wasn't coming from me, and then I heard a voice inside saying, "All will be well," and I believed it. For the first time in decades I dared to hope. By the time I got to the hospital, my throat had started to ease up and the pain became less acute. The ER physician on duty suggested that I follow up with a gastrointestinal doctor to see if I had esophageal spasms. This was the first doctor who actually heard me, saw my pain and didn't tell me, "Chew better." He was adamant about me seeing a gastrointestinal doctor for my choking, which had never been suggested to me before. I went home with a new plan at hand and allowed myself to be cautiously optimistic.

I had found an internal medicine doctor who actually listened. Dr. David Stein, who will now forever be known as my savior, asked about my symptoms, when they had started, how long they had been going on, my complete medical history—you name it. When he was done, he said it sounded like a case of eosinophilic esophagitis. I had never heard of this before. People with severe allergies, which I have, can develop these extra cells that create rings around the esophagus, causing constriction at various points. He described it in detail, and it sounded exactly like what I was experiencing. To know for sure he'd have to do an endoscopy, which would involve putting a camera down my throat and biopsying a piece of my esophagus. We scheduled the procedure for a few weeks later, and again I felt renewed hope. The day of the endoscopy went according to plan. Dr. Stein explained to me that if he did find these rings that were causing restrictions, he would use a balloon at the end of the scope to expand them to prevent future choking instances. That same sense of peace and calm returned, and I felt that I'd finally have answers.

As Dr. Stein predicted, I had developed eosinophilic esophagitis, and he found that the strictures were so severe that my esophagus was only eight millimeters in diameter, whereas the normal size is nearly twice that. No wonder I had been choking all the time. Even he was surprised by how severe a case it was. He used the balloon to increase the size to eleven millimeters and would do another follow-up in six months to get it to within the normal range. I was pretty sore for about a week but otherwise felt fine, and that first bite of food afterwards was glorious!

When I swallowed, it felt like I had the width of a football field for the food to go down.

At the time of this writing, it's been over a decade since I had the procedure done and I haven't choked on anything since! I had never gone more than a month without choking, so this has been a whole new experience for me. Eating is now a joy. I can relax and eat comfortably, knowing that everything will go down as it should.

Now that the acute physical problem was under control, I started to focus on the root cause. Why did I get eosinophilic esophagitis? Where did it come from, and how could I prevent it from recurring? This was a tough process for me, just as it's tough for my clients. Who wants to think that they have something to do with making themselves sick? What I've learned through Reiki, and with hundreds of clients over the years, is that long-term illness starts with a mental or emotional root cause. I started to delve back to the very beginning. The choking incidents started happening when I was about seven years old. What was my life like then? What could have triggered this and set things into motion?

I am the youngest of five kids who grew up in a typical working-class family. The next oldest sibling is six years my senior and the rest are about a year apart. It was hard for me to get my voice out when there was so much competition to be heard. My older siblings were well into preteen dramas by the time I was able to talk. I remember being frustrated because I would have a comment or a question and no one would acknowledge me. I felt patronized even at that young an age. They didn't do it on purpose; they just didn't see me yet as someone that they could converse with. I was always just the little kid. So I didn't say much and kept quiet.

Over the years, in school and other social settings, I didn't speak up, partly because I was unfamiliar with the concept and also because I felt no one would care what I had to say. This did a number on my self-esteem, sending it plunging into the depths of nonexistence. Whenever I had to speak in front of my class, my palms would sweat and my heart would race so fast I thought I would pass out.

This phobia carried over into my professional career. I remember having to give a presentation to a vice president and being so nervous that I scripted the whole presentation. I read my notes verbatim and didn't look up once. It was so bad that my boss reprimanded me afterward. I knew I had to change, or my career would be in jeopardy. I started to practice and slowly but surely gained confidence in speaking in front of larger groups. I rehearsed and rehearsed and knew the material backward and forward. I also tried to make it fun. I realized that if I was having fun, I was less nervous and the content was easier to convey. I started to gain confidence in my work. I knew the material was important and focused on the information I was conveying rather than my fear of getting up and talking in front of people. Over the years I was able to overcome this fear so well that I gave presentations to entire companies that got standing ovations.

This process wasn't an overnight shift. It took years of practiced, focused effort. At the time I didn't have the tools I have now. When I learned Reiki, I incorporated it into my presentations, using it to help with mental focus and clarity for both myself and my audience. Adding Reiki into the mix worked extremely well, even when I had to convey information that was hard to deliver. As I started to teach chakra classes, I began to incorporate more tools and techniques. I found that journaling greatly opens up my throat chakra. When I feel I can't find the right words, writing them down comes much easier. I also call upon Archangel Gabriel to help me speak and convey the right messages, whether I'm teaching a class, having a client session or delivering a presentation.

I can't say with 100 percent certainty that I'm *cured*, but I can say that now I have tools and knowledge to help better understand why my throat seizes up. Understanding the why and addressing it through journaling, prayer, affirmations and other techniques allows my voice to come through so that it no longer feels the need to tighten up and shut down.

How Do We Get Unstuck?

Finding Your Voice

I've found that one of the most effective ways of clearing the throat chakra is by journaling. Writing down how you truly feel without fear of judgment or ridicule can be tremendously liberating. When you take the time to look inward and put pen to paper or fingers to keyboard you will be amazed at what comes out. You might have memories and feelings that are long forgotten and then they suddenly appear on the page. Think of journaling as a way of purging your physical body from the pent-up emotions that you've been harboring for years. Once done, you can ceremoniously burn the journal as a way of closing that chapter in your life.

Writing letters can be another helpful tool for finding your voice and expressing yourself. If you have someone in your life, whether past or present, that you feel you aren't able to communicate with, write them a letter. You don't have to give it to them if you choose not to; what's more important is the feeling that you are able to get the words out.

Seeing a therapist is another great way to help you find your voice. A trained mental health professional can provide a safe, nonjudgmental environment where you can unearth and explore emotions you might not even be aware of. As with any practitioner, trust your intuition as to whether that person is the right match for you.

Building Your Confidence

Most of my clients who have blocks in their throat chakras feel uncomfortable speaking in public. Pushing yourself out of your comfort zone and signing up for public speaking classes at a local community college or adult education center can provide you with the tools and confidence you need to speak in public.

As mentioned previously, whenever I gave a presentation, I would rehearse the material so that I felt 100 percent confident. I'd also visualize how I wanted the presentation to go, whom I'd like to be in the room and the response I'd like to get from the audience. Once I started employing this method, I was taken aback by the complete transformations that took place. The audience became more engaged, they were attentive and asked questions and the material fostered additional debate and action steps.

Unleashing Your Creative Side

If you feel creatively blocked, take out a sheet of paper and a pencil and just let your hand move across the page. You can doodle, draw circles, spirals, squares, whatever you are in the mood for. You can get a coloring book and color. You can take out a paint brush and canvas and let your mood pick the colors and shapes you draw. Pick up your guitar or drumsticks and just rattle around for a while. It doesn't have to be perfect—far from it; it should be whatever you're in the mood for. Whatever you feel like putting down on paper or playing on an instrument is the right choice. Remove any judgment or fear of imperfections. This is just an exercise to get the creative juices flowing again.

Have fun, be creative and try whatever feels most comfortable for you. Don't force it. You'll know when you're on the right path.

* * *

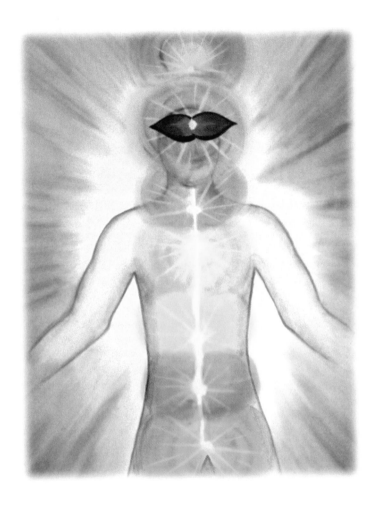

Chapter Nine

Third Eye Chakra: Seeing with Clarity

Defined

The third eye chakra governs our ability to see things clearly. Often drawn as an eye with a cobalt blue iris looking back at you, it is where we store our sixth sense, our psychic ability, our clairvoyance. The third eye chakra is located in the middle of the forehead in between the eyebrows and is also known as the brow chakra. It is one of the higher chakras, which focus more on the spiritual aspects of our being and less on our earthly, physical needs.

What It Affects

A blocked or imbalanced third eye chakra can lead to feelings of loss and confusion with regard to our purpose here on earth, relationships, and career. It can reduce or eliminate our ability to see the truth and prevent us from using our sixth sense to gain deeper meaning and knowledge of the spiritual world. On the physical side, it can affect us with headaches as severe as migraines and can leave us feeling mentally cloudy and unable to focus.

Most of us who have issues with our third eye are unable to make decisions. We may feel stuck and lost in one or more areas of our life. When this chakra is clear and in balance, we can clearly see our path and the steps we need to take. The third eye also holds the key to our psychic ability, which can open up greatly when this chakra is in balance and clear.

Why We Get Stuck

All of us are born with psychic gifts. Some of these gifts include a *gut sense*, or *knowing* that something is about to happen. Some of them include being able to see and hear things others cannot. Some of us can feel things profoundly. For instance, have you ever walked into a place, maybe a historical site or an old museum or concert hall, and felt that you needed to leave for reasons you can't explain? Have you had vivid dreams about things that later happen in real life? Or do you remember having imaginary friends as children that seemed as real as your parents growing up? These are all signs of the types of psychic gifts we can possess. Some of us are more in tune with these gifts than others.

There are several reasons why the third eye can get blocked, the main culprit is fear. We are afraid of what people would think of us if we were to express our psychic gifts. Would we be outcasts or ostracized? Would people think we are crazy? Would *we* think we were crazy?

We may also be afraid of what we might experience if we were to open ourselves up to these gifts. Will we start to see, hear or feel things that are scary? Will we be able to control these gifts and turn them off when we want? Or is psychic ability like a Pandora's Box: once opened, we can never close it again?

Some might find it difficult to reconcile these gifts with their religious beliefs. Psychic senses can be misinterpreted as *occult* and can have negative connotations. If we were to open up our psychic senses, would we be violating our own religious beliefs? Is there room in our belief system for science, religion and these psychic gifts to coexist?

Client Stories

When Giselle came to see me, she was experiencing blackouts at work and was currently on medical leave from her hospital administrative job. The doctors couldn't find anything conclusively wrong with her and diagnosed her with hyperthyroidism. She was under a tremendous amount of stress at work, and it inhibited her ability to focus. Physically she felt pressure in her forehead and tightness in her stomach and was constantly tired even after a good night's sleep.

When I first started working with Giselle I was immediately drawn to her third eye, her heart and her adrenal glands. I could feel energetically how her stress was tied to her inability to see things clearly and being able to focus. Her job required her to be on call 24/7. This constant stress meant that she was in a constant state of alert and could never relax or have any down time. Not only was her job demanding, but it took an emotional toll as well. She would be thrust into difficult situations which involved her having to let staff go. She knew she had to find a different line of work but didn't know what to do.

After the first few sessions the tension in her forehead would diminish. When it did, she began to see things more clearly. She reported seeing bright white lights during our Reiki sessions. She would also get images of becoming a mom and raising two children in the future. Giselle also came to the conclusion that she could no longer work at her current job and that being in an office wasn't for her. She wanted to work in nature.

Giselle became a Reiki practitioner, and as she used Reiki on herself, more things became clear. She became aware that she was an empath, absorbing other people's energy and emotions. With Reiki, she was able to protect and clear her energy, freeing herself from other people's dramas. The more we worked together and she worked on herself, the more guidance she began to receive and the more she reconnected with her spiritual side.

How Do We Get Unstuck?

Self-Evaluation

The third eye is a higher frequency chakra, one that is more closely aligned to the spiritual plane than the earthly plane. Given that, it is important for us to first address our earthly or lower chakra needs before we can successfully pursue a clear and charged third eye. For instance, will we be able to further develop our psychic gifts if we're concerned about our physical safety or our financial security (root chakra)? Will we be able to focus on opening up our psychic gifts if we're insecure and lack confidence in ourselves (solar plexus)?

102

So my first advice in starting to work on your third eye chakra is to first ask yourself, "do I feel safe, loved, secure? Do I have confidence in myself? Can I fully express myself?" If you answered yes, then you're ready to work on your third eye. Even if you answered no you can still work on your third eye, but it might take a bit more time and energy.

Finding Your Inner Guidance System

Opening up your third eye chakra allows you to see the world more clearly. Think of all the decisions you have to make in life and how much easier those decisions would be if you could see the situation and outcome clearly. How would your life change if you knew for certain that you had picked the right school, the right partner, the right job? How much stress would fade away because you knew which direction your life needed to take?

Quiet reflection and meditation can provide you with the stillness needed to hear that inner guide directing you on your path. There is a famous story of a guru leaving his students after several decades of teaching. He said he had taught them all he knew and that they needed to move forward and become their own gurus. He meant for them to become their own lighthouses instead of relying on him for all the answers. *For in the end, all the answers that we seek can be found within.* Too often we look for external sources to provide us with answers when the true source for knowledge lies inside us. We just need to tune in to hear it.

The quickest and easiest method to tap into our own inner guidance system is a technique I call body check. I will have my clients sit quietly and take a few deep breaths. I might have them focus on their breathing or on releasing any tension in their muscles. This takes just a minute or two. The purpose is to help them relax and clear their mind. Next, I'll rephrase the question that they are seeking answers to. For example, "You are with the person that you will be with for the rest of your life." Then I'll ask them to see if they notice any physical changes. Do they begin to breathe faster? Do they notice any tension popping up anywhere? Or are they at peace? Then I'll have them focus on their breathing again to get them back to neutral. After a few minutes, I'll then state the reverse: "The person you are with is not the person you will be with for the rest of your life." Then I'll check in with them again and see how their body feels. This method has proven to be effective time and time again. When your body relaxes, you know that is the direction you need to go. When your body tenses up, then you know someone or something is not right for you.

Another way to approach this is to ask a question that requires a yes or no response. For example, I could ask, "Do you want to be with this person for the rest of your life - yes or no?" And the first answer that comes to them is the right answer. Try it out, don't over think it and don't second-guess yourself. Trust that what comes is the right answer.

Raising Your Vibration

As you begin to work with higher frequency energies, you may notice certain things in your diet becoming difficult to digest or negative people or toxic places becoming difficult for you to be around. This is because higher and lower frequencies cannot coexist in harmony. Do not be surprised if you begin to find dairy or red meat hard on the system. Things that you used to like might become less enjoyable. You might also find that certain people in your life drift away as you continue to work on yourself. Don't be alarmed if this happens. This is a natural and safe progression in your development. This is your body's way of telling you what's OK and what's not OK for you as you start to move closer to your true self. Employ the body-check method mentioned previously to help determine what things in your life are not working well for you.

Meditation is key to raising your vibration. It allows you to open and unblock the third eye and the crown chakras. I talk in more detail about meditation in the next chapter. In this chapter, I'll discuss a meditation that is specific to opening up the third eye chakra.

Find a quiet space where you are comfortable and won't be disturbed for at least ten or fifteen minutes. You can play soothing music in the background if you'd like. If you have an amethyst crystal, you can use it in this meditation by holding it in your hand or by placing it gently on your forehead if you are lying down. Close your eyes and draw your attention to your forehead, just above where your eyebrows meet. As you focus your attention there you might start to feel a tingling or a pressure. That's good, and means you are increasing the energy and blood flow to the area. Keep it up! Next, using your imagination, visualize a closed eye in front of you. As you focus on this eye, the lid slowly opens to show you a cobalt blue eye looking back at you. Hold the image of this opened eye as long as you can and repeat these affirmations:

* I can see clearly.
* I am following my inner guidance system.
* All the answers I seek lie within.

After a few more minutes, bring your attention back to your breathing and then return to full consciousness. This is a good time to grab a journal and start writing down any feelings or sensations you had during the meditation. This is also the time to ask yourself the questions that you are seeking answers to.

Clearing and Shielding Your Energy

As you begin to develop your psychic gifts, you'll need to employ one or more techniques to keep your energy clear and free from lower energy. If you discovered that you are an empath like Giselle, there are a number of effective tools you can use to help shield and clear your energy. The easiest one is to envision a white light bubble completely surrounding you, almost as if you're inside a big egg. Believe that the white light will protect you and that nothing can penetrate it except light and love. Any negative or lower energy will simply bounce off. For my clients that are empathic, I suggest they do this as soon as they wake up in the morning and have the intention that it stay with them throughout their day.

Another method I find useful is employing black tourmaline crystal. The vibrational pattern and frequency of this crystal turn it into a sponge so that it absorbs the energy in the room instead of you. I suggest you get a crystal big enough to handle the negative energy in your environment; for smaller issues, one that fits in your pocket would be fine. If you can somehow wear the crystal or have it on your person, even better! Make sure you clear it out on a regular basis.[9]

Taking weekly sea salt baths will also clear your energy. This method removes energy from your system that doesn't belong to you. Most New Age shops have sea salt, follow the instructions for use. Most suggest 1/2 to 1 full cup of sea salt per bath. And make sure the water is warm enough to absorb the salt. Soak for a minimum of 20 minutes with the intention of clearing and removing energy that is not yours.

* * *

[9] See Chapter Seven: Heart Chakra, p. 82.

Chapter Ten

Crown Chakra:
The Spiritual Self

Defined

The crown chakra is located on top of the head. It is the highest chakra, with a higher vibration than the lower, more earthly chakras. The crown chakra focuses on our connection to our higher self, the divine, universal consciousness and God. It is where we connect to our spirituality and our spiritual self. It embodies the place we go when we achieve inner peace through meditation, yoga, and similar practices. It is where we can achieve enlightenment and nirvana.

What It Affects

Our crown chakra is tied to our pineal gland, which regulates aging, sleep, reproductive timing, puberty and menopause and can cause headaches, migraines and nervous disorders such as epilepsy, paralysis, Parkinson's disease and high blood pressure.

Why We Get Stuck

People who have difficulty connecting to their higher self or feel lost spiritually will have issues with their crown chakra as a result. Negative religious experiences or lack of spiritual beliefs can cause this chakra to shut down. If you are lost in your thoughts, chasing one thought to the next, unable to find peace, your spirit will be unable to rest, making it difficult to connect to your higher, spiritual self.

It can be difficult to achieve a state of spiritual growth when our lower chakras, our earthly needs, are not being met. As mentioned in Chapter Four: Root Chakra, spirituality and inner peace were low on the priority list for the homeless women worried about how they were going to survive. It can also be challenging to become spiritually open when we lack confidence in ourselves (solar plexus) or are unable to express ourselves fully (throat chakra). Therefore it is recommended that you work on the lower chakras first in order to achieve greater success with the crown chakra.

Much like the third eye chakra, a healthy crown chakra allows us to hear our own inner guidance and trust our spiritual path. The crown chakra is also where we can receive messages from God, angels and our spirit guides.

Client Stories

One of my clients whom I'm happy to now call my friend first came to me back in 2011. Anna came to me because she was just *off*. She had the normal stresses of a mother with a young child and wanted to give Reiki a try to see what it could do for her. During her first session, I noticed her taking in quite a bit of Reiki in her solar plexus area and her throat chakras. When we discussed it after her session, she admitted to giving a lot of advice to others, leaving her feeling drained. I suggested that she learn Reiki for herself so that she can give advice and help others without draining her own energy. She jumped at the chance and signed up for a Reiki I and II class that next weekend.

Reiki resonated strongly with Anna, and she became sensitive to the energy around and through her. During her next session, I noticed quite a change in her energy. She wasn't taking in as much energy as before, and I noticed the Reiki was now focused higher up in her third eye and crown chakras. I could feel the Reiki working in her, cleaning out one chakra at a time and moving up to the next one.

She came to see me frequently as different events in her life popped up. For instance, her father-in-law was coming to stay with them for a six-month period. She was apprehensive about this as her father-in-law was highly critical and demanding of her, and I could feel her heart, throat and solar plexus taking in a lot of energy during those sessions. We talked about how she needed to come from a place of compassion (heart chakra) when dealing with him and how she needed to be strong and stand up for herself (solar plexus chakra), feeling confident and comfortable expressing her thoughts and needs (throat chakra). She admitted to feeling a knot in the pit of her stomach when she thought about her father-in-law. Her throat chakra also became affected during this time because she felt she had to hold her tongue in order to maintain peace in her house.

As we continued to heal the lower chakras, her crown chakra started to become more active, helping to clear out the negative thoughts and replace them with a new perspective. Anna was able to see her situation from an outsider's vantage point and distance herself from the negative environment so that it no longer affected her. She became an observer in her own story, rising above the conflict and seeing everyone involved as divine souls who were also struggling to find peace within themselves.

When meeting each obstacle in her life, she learned through Reiki to find clarity and peace in her current situation and a clear path in which to overcome them. She was able to move beyond the situation to a loving perspective, allowing her to grow and to learn. She began to trust herself and her place in the universe. I am humbled by her transformation over the course of just a few years. Anna's divine self shines through inspiring others to find their own light.

How Do We Get Unstuck?

Finding the Higher Connection

The most effective way for us to work on our crown chakras is through meditation. When we can find that stillness of mind, we open ourselves up to a direct line of communication with our higher selves, God and angels. Meditation can take many shapes and forms. It does not necessarily require hours upon hours of silent reflection. Meditating for even five minutes can greatly impact your overall health and well-being.

Sit in a quiet, comfortable space where you will not be interrupted and simply breathe. Listen to your breath. Count your heartbeats if you need your mind to focus on something. If thoughts pop up gently bring your focus back to your breathing. Check in with your body and see what it's telling you. How do your toes feel? How do your calves and knees feel? How about your elbows, hips and lower back? Do a quick inventory of your body, section by section, and if you notice any tension or discomfort, breathe in, bringing oxygen into those areas then release the tension as you exhale.

If you find it difficult to get your mind to stop running like a hamster in a wheel, then try guided meditation. You can find great resources for this online, I have a few posted on my YouTube channel found on my website, reiki-energyhealing.com. One of my favorites, especially for chakra work, is Doreen Virtue's Chakra Clearing guided meditation.[10] She has two meditations that she guides you through, one for the morning and one for the evening. It's a great way to start and finish your day.

Another form of meditation is to practice being present in any given situation. For instance, while you're making your coffee or tea in the morning, let your mind focus only on that task. As you sit down to drink it, tune in to how it feels in your hands, the shape of the mug, the taste, the smell—go through all your senses. Remove thoughts about how you're going to tackle your day or what's ahead; simply drink and enjoy the sensations.

Practicing yoga is a fantastic way to help clear out and charge all chakras and prepare the body and mind for meditation. Did you know that the main point

---

[10] Doreen Virtue, *Chakra Clearing* (Carlsbad, CA: Hay House, 1997).

of yoga is the meditation at the very end? Yoga is a way for us to charge up and clear the mind and body so that we can achieve stillness at the end of the practice. Make sure you listen to your body and don't force yourself into positions your body isn't comfortable with.

Look for Signs
Once you are ready to truly expand your spirit and open your crown chakra, you'll notice opportunities presenting themselves almost magically. A spiritual teacher may give a lecture in your neighborhood, or you may be invited to participate in a meditation or yoga group or you may be given a book from a friend that introduces you to a new way of thinking. You might also come across opportunities to be of service to others, to learn, to grow, to teach.

When you reach this state in your spiritual development, serendipity becomes the norm. You'll be constantly amazed by the miracles that take place in your life. Manifestation will become second nature. Healing will be a constant state. Opening up and becoming aware of your surroundings will lead you down new, exciting paths. Enjoy it, trust and surrender and you will find inner peace and a divine sense of self.

* * *

Bunnie at her granddaughter's wedding, May 2013

Chapter Eleven

Bunnie

A few years into my Reiki practice, I received an email from a woman in Southern California who wanted me to give Reiki to her elderly mother. Her mother was recently diagnosed with stomach cancer and was frail and unable to eat and maintain her weight. I jumped at the chance to help a cancer patient and started working with Bridget, or "Bunnie" as she was lovingly known, on a weekly basis.

When I first met Bunnie I was struck by just how frail she was. I was a bit worried about my ability to maintain my composure, feeling tears well up in my eyes as I looked at her. But then she opened her mouth and gave me a beaming smile and greeted me hello with a thick Irish accent, making me feel instantly at ease. I quickly learned that it was her body that was frail, not her spirit.

Over the course of six months I grew to love our sessions together. Bunnie was a spitfire of energy, all 80 pounds of her. She always wore a huge smile and asked about my kittens and my husband in her thick Irish brogue. She had such a caring heart that sometimes I'd catch myself unburdening myself to her and then had to stop and remember, "Hey, she's here to be well and not here to listen to my problems!" She was just that type of person.

The effects that the Reiki had on her were immediate. Her nausea dissipated, her appetite returned and she gradually started to gain weight again—not much, but even a pound or two was a huge improvement. The Reiki helped to show how her constant worrying might be fueling her cancer and that a shift toward prayer and giving her worries to God would help. Reiki brought her a sense of peace and comfort and helped her regain her energy, allowing her to return to the volunteer work at the church that she loved so much. She was also able to attend her granddaughter's wedding, which involved a week-long celebration including entertaining family from her native Ireland. Early on I had attuned her to the first level of Reiki so that she could give Reiki to herself whenever she felt the need. And after six months, her scans could find no trace of the tumors. She was cancer-free!

Over the course of our sessions together I began to feel a great sense of gratitude. I was emotionally invested in Bunnie. I always try to connect with my clients on an emotional and spiritual level, but this was different. With Bunnie I felt like I was treating my own mother. And there were quite a few similarities: Bunnie was Catholic, like my mom, and fighting an aggressive cancer, like my mom, and had raised five children (four girls and one boy), like my mom and was a constant worrier over her children, much like my mom. But I never gave Reiki to my mom because I learned it after she had passed away. Do I think she would still be alive if I had been able to give her Reiki? I'm not sure, I don't think so, but I know the Reiki would have brought her peace and comfort during the difficult days. And for that I do have some regret. Being able to give this beautiful healing gift to a woman who reminded me so much of my own mother and what she went through made me feel complete, as if things had come full circle. I was healing myself by being able to give Reiki to Bunnie because I was able to help someone else's mother when I couldn't help my own.

Then Bunnie passed quickly and suddenly. She had gone to an appointment for an ultrasound after complaining of pain in her stomach. During the ultrasound she felt even more excruciating pain and was admitted to the hospital. She died just a few days later, surrounded by her children, grandchildren and her loving husband Jack.

I was devastated, as if I had lost my mother again. She was doing so well that it was a shock. She had developed these pains in her stomach, and her doctors had assured her that it was an ulcer due to the radiation treatments she'd received.

I wasn't able to attend Bunnie's service. I had a Reiki class scheduled for that day and felt that Bunnie would have wanted me to pass the torch on and initiate others.

Toward the end of every class, I have my students give me a Reiki session as a learning exercise. During this session I felt someone holding my left hand, long after my students had moved on. At one point it became very strong and I looked and no one was there. Then I got a very quick flash of Bunnie holding my hand, smiling down on me. I was deeply moved and started to cry. My students didn't notice and the one student that had held that same hand previously mentioned how she saw bright pink when she was holding that hand, which is a sign of love.

I can feel Bunnie's presence around me, especially when I'm working on the elderly or with other cancer patients. She sends me butterflies to let me know she's nearby.

Bunnie would always bring me holiday greeting cards—Christmas cards, Easter cards and Valentine's Day cards. I still have her Valentine's Day card on my desk at my office. It states, "Love is what you do. Love is what you are." In a phrase, that captures Reiki, my experience working with it and working with others. Reiki is love. It is sharing unconditional love with others. Helping them remember how to be well again by loving themselves. Reminding them that they are connected to the universal love and that they are worthy of it.

May you be inspired to be well as I send you Reiki love.

* * *

Acknowledgments

This book would not be possible without the loving support of my husband Causey. Thank you for being there and helping me with every step of the process.

Special thanks to Dawn Warren for lending her amazing talents, Beth Partin for her keen eyes and to all my Reiki teachers, students and clients, past, present and future, to my loving family and friends, to all the great folks at Harborside Health Center in San Jose, California, to the Breast Cancer Connection in Palo Alto, California, and to the InnVision Homeless Network in San Jose, California.

Without your love, help, support and stories, this book wouldn't be possible. Thank you for everything.

* * *

About the Author

Francie has been practicing and teaching Reiki professionally since 2009. She has personally given thousands of Reiki sessions and has worked in medical clinics, cancer centers and homeless shelters. She teaches all levels of Reiki including additional workshops on Psychic Development, Angels, Chakras and more.

Francie has a B.A. in Interdisciplinary Studies from U.C. Berkeley where she studied sociology, anthropology and physics. Francie worked for nearly two decades as a market researcher and data analyst for several high-tech companies such as Macromedia, Yahoo and Facebook.

She has been married for over twenty years to the love of her life and co-owns and runs their comic book store Black Cat Comics. Francie has a black belt in Tae Kwon Do and likes to play the drums and mother her kittens.

You can reach her at:

whyareyousick.net
whyareyousick

Made in United States
Orlando, FL
23 May 2022

18120542R00080